CONTINUING
THE DIALOGUE

**A Pastoral Study Document
of the House of Bishops
to the Church as the
Church Considers
Issues of Human Sexuality**

**with discussion guide
prepared by
The Committee for Dialogue
on Human Sexuality**

MEMBERS OF THE A104sa COMMITTEE

The Rt. Rev. Richard F. Grein, *Chair*
The Rt. Rev. Frank K. Allan
The Rt. Rev. Mark Dyer
The Rt. Rev. C. Christopher Epting
The Rt. Rev. Rogers S. Harris
The Rt. Rev. Richard L. Shimpfky
The Rt. Rev. Harry W. Shipps
The Rt. Rev. Vincent W. Warner
The Rev. Jane N. Garrett
The Rev. Barnum McCarty
The Rev. Warner T. Traynham
Mrs. Kit T. Caffey
J.P. Causey, Esq.
Ms. Mary Meader

© 1995, Forward Movement Publications
412 Sycamore Street
Cincinnati, Ohio 45202-4195

FOREWORD FROM THE COMMITTEE

The title given to this Pastoral Study Document states in a succinct way what the document is all about: *Continuing the Dialogue: A Pastoral Study Document of the House of Bishops to the Church as the Church Considers Issues of Human Sexuality.*

The committee charged with writing this Pastoral Study Document recognized early in our discussions that while we agreed on the great majority of issues connected with human sexuality, there were several issues which could not be resolved by even the most carefully written statement.

The persons making up the committee, eight Bishops and six members of the House of Deputies, are united in a common faith; on the central affirmations of creed and sacraments, we are joined together. On the subject at hand, we represent a broad spectrum of viewpoints and experience which we know to be representative of the Church as a whole. But within this difference of perspective we shared a common attitude—willingness to listen to one another even on potentially divisive issues. This openness allowed us to come to some level of appreciation of perspectives that differed from our own. What we learned from this experience we want to pass on to the Church.

Whereas the solution to our dilemmas lay beyond our ability to grasp, we discovered we could remain together as a community in dialogue sharing common faith. This Pastoral Study Document then is not intended to offer a particular solution or some new unusual perspective on the issues, nor have we changed the present teaching of this Church on any of these issues. At the same time, we do have a clear purpose: to encourage a process of dialogue and to remind the Church that our strength is what we share through our common baptismal covenant.

Thus what we hope to teach is about a way for this Church to work together as it seeks a common mind under the guidance of the Holy Spirit. In this teaching we have also tried objectively to provide a history of our Church's discussions on human sexuality, the traditional Christian teaching on matters of human sexuality and marriage, differing perspectives by biblical theologians on key Scripture references, and a description of what the 1991 General Convention called "discontinuities." We have also offered a set of guidelines for our life together as we seek answers to these important concerns so that when we are asked, "Where does the Episcopal Church stand on issues of human sexuality?" we can reply—we stand together seeking God's guidance.

Finally, the appendix contains a report from Bishop O'Kelly Whitaker's committee, which guided the many discussions on human sexuality. While those discussions are not to be considered a referendum, the report offers many valuable insights on attitudes held by Episcopalians. Importantly, it appears that most found the discussion helpful and productive.

The committee was conscious from the beginning that it worked for the House of Bishops. What we wrote was theirs to accept or reject. Altogether we produced five drafts with opportunities for the Bishops to offer reflections and critiques and make the document their own. Throughout the process this Pastoral Study Document was reviewed by ethicists and biblical scholars. We were pleased to be able to use their many suggestions to improve the Document. On the subject of human sexuality, even the so-called experts do not agree.

In preparing this Pastoral Study Document, we were mindful that its purpose, in the last analysis, is to assist persons, in whatever their life circumstances, to live as faithful Christians, growing and deepening in their life with Christ. Nothing for Christians can take the place of a strong life of prayer, the study of Scripture, and participation in the liturgical and communal life of the Church. In every area of human life, God calls us to fidelity in our relationships—with God, with one another in the community of the Church, in our personal lives.

As this Pastoral Study Document makes evident, devoted Christians in our faith community do not find themselves of a single mind on various aspects of our lives as sexual beings. All the more reason, then, for congregations and other gatherings of Episcopalians to struggle together, as we have and as the House of Bishops has, to listen for the voice of the Holy Spirit in the midst of our life together, seeking forgiveness from one another and from God for the ways in which deeply held emotions often block genuine listening. What we must not do as we make this journey together is question any one's faith commitment even when we disagree with their position on these concerns. We must, as as the poet Rilke said, "learn to live the question, and perhaps one day we will live into the answer."

The Rt. Rev. Richard F. Grein, Chair

CONTENTS

CONTINUING
THE DIALOGUE

1
THE DIALOGUE TO DATE IN THE EPISCOPAL CHURCH

Introduction

Issues related to human sexuality are high on the agenda of virtually every Christian denomination in our day. There are many reasons for this, of which the sexual revolution of the sixties and seventies and the women's movement are but two. The relative silence of the Church on matters sexual in the past and the current wellness and spiritual-growth movements in the Church have also played their part. When the power and centrality of sexuality in our lives and its close association with spirituality and the desire for intimacy with God and one another are added, it is no wonder that issues of human sexuality are so prominent in the Church today.

Of all the issues related to human sexuality, one has occupied a central place in the entire discussion. Largely as a result of the emergence of the gay liberation movement, homosexuality (and specifically the debates surrounding the blessing of gay and lesbian unions and the ordination of noncelibate gay and lesbian persons) has played a key role in the discussion by forcing us to look again at the meaning and role of sexuality in general.

Certainly this has been the case for the Episcopal Church in the United States of America. The 70th General Convention, meeting in Phoenix, Arizona, in July of 1991, acknowledged its inability to resolve the complex issues surrounding human sexuality by means of the normal legislative process. The Convention opted instead for a process of continued study and dialogue across the whole Church before the 71st General

1

Convention to be held in Indianapolis, Indiana, during the summer of 1994. One part of this process called for congregational and diocesan dialogues, the results of which were to be reported back through the Provincial structures.[1] A second part mandated the preparation of a Pastoral Teaching of the House of Bishops prior to the 71st General Convention. A rehearsal of events leading up to this process may be instructive.

Background, 1976–1991

At least as far back as the 1976 General Convention, resolutions passed by the bishops and deputies began to frame the parameters of the debate. One resolution acknowledged "that homosexual persons are children of God who have a full and equal claim with all other persons upon the love, acceptance and pastoral concern and care of the Church." In 1977, at a special meeting in Port St. Lucie, Florida, the House of Bishops accepted the report of its Commission on Theology, which stated, "The Church is right to confine its nuptial blessing exclusively to heterosexual marriage. Homosexual unions witness to incompleteness." It further stated, "In the case of an advocating and/ or practicing homosexual," ordination is inadmissible because, "It involves the Church in a public denial of its own theological and moral norms on sexuality," and because, "it would require the Church's sanction of such a life style, not only as acceptable but worthy of emulation." In 1979, the 66th General Convention adopted a resolution recommending that those having authority in the ordination process recognize:

1. There are many human conditions, some of them in the area of sexuality, which bear upon a person's suitability for ordination;

2. Every ordinand is expected to lead a life which is "a wholesome example to all people" (Book of Common Prayer, pp. 517, 532, 544).[2] There should be no barrier to the ordination of qualified persons of either heterosexual or homosexual orientation whose behavior the Church considers wholesome;

3. [T]he traditional teaching of the Church on marriage, marital fidelity, and sexual chastity [is] the standard of Christian sexual morality. Candidates for ordination are expected to conform to this standard. Therefore, . . . it is not appropriate for this Church to ordain a practicing homosexual, or any person who is engaged in heterosexual relations outside of marriage.

However, an indication of some real division at least in the House of Bishops was shown by the inclusion of a minority report signed in 1979 by 20 bishops and in 1988 by 29 (out of 175). While joining their fellow bishops in affirming marriage and celibacy as appropriate vocations, these bishops also affirmed the "ministries of ordained persons known to be homosexual. . . ." They also declared, "Not all of these persons have been celibate; and in the relationships of many of them, maintained in the face of social hostility and against great odds, we have seen a redeeming quality which in its way and according to its mode is no less a sign to the world of God's love than is the more usual sign of Christian marriage."

The report went on to state,

[W]here an ideally stable relationship has not, or has not yet, been achieved, we are conscious of ordained homosexual persons who are wrestling responsibly, and in the fear of God, with the Christian implications of their sexuality and who seek to be responsible, caring, and non-exploitive people even in the occasionally transient relationships which the hostility of our society toward homosexual persons . . . makes inevitable.

The minority rejected the idea that "either homosexual orientation as such" or "the responsible and self-giving use of such a mode of sexuality, constitutes a scandal in and of itself." Since their examination of Scripture gave "no certain basis for a total or absolute condemnation of either homosexual persons or homosexual activities . . ." they stated their inability to accept the 66th Convention's recommendation on ordination and instead affirmed their intention to exclude no person on the basis of a category but to select each candidate for ordination on the basis of individual merit, "as a whole human being and in the light of the particular circumstances obtaining in this case."

Such a position made a debate not only on homosexuality but on sexuality in general inevitable. For its part, the Standing Commission on Health and Human Affairs sought to encourage and inform the discussion in both areas. (This Commission, made up of members from both Houses, is an Interim Body of General Convention. The reports and recommendations of Interim Bodies have no standing unless or until they are adopted by the Convention. The Commission's reports are cited in this review because they are representative of some of the perspectives in the discussion.) In its report to the 1988 Convention, the Commission cited significant changes in society as one reason for the need to review sexual standards. It reaffirmed marriage as the standard or norm in which human sexuality is to be shared and at the same time acknowledged disagreement in its ranks as to whether sexual intimacy in any other relationship can be called "moral." It noted that "the majority of our Church is committed to an attempt to call the society to the traditional sexual standards. A significant minority, however, of this Church is convinced that the time has come to begin a process that will enable Christians to think through new moral and sexual options in the light of new realities."

With respect to homosexuality, however, the report specifically avoided making any legislative recommendations. Instead, it confessed to the complexity and lack of clarity of the issue and suggested that a greater measure of openness and understanding were required before the Church could confidently make any ultimate moral judgments. The Commission urged the Church to create a context in which it could listen to homosexual persons tell their stories and in which they would feel comfortable in doing so. It observed that although many heterosexual Christians say, when speaking of homosexuals, we must "hate the sin and love the sinner," homosexual Christians almost consistently report feelings of being hated rather than loved by their fellow Episcopalians.

Finally, 52 bishops at the 1988 General Convention signed a copy of a statement from the 1987 Synod of the Church of England and asked that it be included in the Convention Journal. The statement read, in part:

> This Synod [of the Church of England] affirms the biblical and traditional teaching on chastity and fidelity in personal relationships is a response to and expression of God's love for each of us, and in particular affirms:
>
> 1. that sexual intercourse is an act of total commitment which belongs properly within a permanent marriage relationship;
>
> 2. that fornication and adultery are sins against this ideal, and are to be met by a call to repentance and the exercise of compassion;

3.   that homosexual acts also fall short of this ideal, and are likewise to be met by a call to repentance and the exercise of compassion.

4.   that all Christians are called to be exemplary in all spheres of morality, including sexual morality, and that holiness of life is particularly required for Christian leaders.

Authority and Collegiality

Believing that the 1979 and 1988 resolutions regarding the "inappropriateness" of ordaining noncelibate homosexuals to be recommendatory in nature and therefore lacking canonical authority, the Rt. Rev. John S. Spong, with the consent of the Standing Committee of the Diocese of Newark, and after written notification to the Presiding Bishop and the House of Bishops, ordained the Rev. Robert Williams, "a homosexual person living in a public, avowed relationship with a person of the same sex" to the priesthood in 1990. Following this ordination, the Presiding Bishop and his Council of Advice reaffirmed the content of the 1979 resolution of the General Convention declaring the ordination of "a practicing homosexual or any other person who is engaged in heterosexual relations outside of marriage" to be inappropriate. This statement was then reaffirmed by the House of Bishops meeting in Washington, DC, in September of 1990.

The main focus of the statement, however, was the authority of the General Convention resolutions and the accountability of bishops within the Church. The conflict over sexuality had now also become an issue of authority and collegiality. Those affirming the statement voted to disassociate themselves, not from the gay and lesbian members of the Church, but from the actions of the Standing Committee and the Bishop of Newark in carrying out this ordination contrary to the stated mind of the Church.

In an attempt to provide healing and some measure of reconciliation in the wake of these events, the House of Bishops, still meeting in Washington, DC, released a statement calling the Episcopal Church to dialogue and patience. The bishops once again acknowledged their division on the issues and urged the Church to respond to the call of the 1988 General Convention to disciplined dialogue. "We call on you," they wrote, "to share our recognition of the inherent faithlessness of a closed mind, one that blocks God from illuminating old truths in a fresh way, from calling us to new understandings or from leading us into new ways of thinking."

The 70th General Convention, 1991

Two other highly publicized ordinations of noncelibate homosexuals (in the Diocese of Washington and the Diocese of Newark), and a number of other such ordinations carried out with less publicity, escalated the concerns or hopes of many throughout the Episcopal Church in 1991. It was in this climate that the bishops and deputies gathered for the 70th General Convention in Phoenix during the summer of 1991. In preparation for that meeting, the Commission on Human Affairs had submitted its report summarizing the results of diocesan dialogues to date and making recommendations based upon the Commission's own study of these issues. Although this commission report was never approved, many of the issues it raised are pertinent to an understanding of the ongoing debate.

In its report, the Commission noted that only 28 of the 99 dioceses had submitted reports on the commended dialogue during the triennium, leading to the conclusion that fewer than half the dioceses complied with the recommendation of the General Convention. It noted that no strong consensus had emerged in the dialogues, although there was considerable agreement on the need for the Church to provide leadership in this area. Turning to its own deliberations, the Commission agreed that while sexual desire can often be misused, the Church needs to emphasize the positive aspects of the fact that we are sexual beings. It agreed that sex is rightly used in Christian marriage and rejected sexual exploitation of the powerless by the powerful. It agreed that homosexual orientation is not culpable or inconsistent with being a Christian and opposed the argument that genuine conversion for gays always involves a transformation to a heterosexual orientation. It agreed that human beings are not meant to be alone "and that homosexual relationships often provide such comfort and support and exhibit commendable love and commitment." It agreed that homophobia (the irrational fear of homosexuals) is widespread in both our culture and the Church and should be rooted out. It reaffirmed the 1985 Convention's call for dialogue to better understand homosexual persons and dispel myths about homosexuality.

Finally, a majority of the Commission made two recommendations: "That the Standing Liturgical Commission study the theological and liturgical issues involved in affirming and blessing these covenants of gay and lesbian persons and begin the process of developing liturgical forms for them."[3]

Further, a majority of the Commission recommended, "That the Church acknowledge that it has for centuries ordained gay men and has in recent years ordained lesbians from whose ministries it has benefited, and that some of these persons have been and are sexually active" and

> [T]hat the Church be open to ordaining gay men and lesbians otherwise qualified who display the same integrity in their sexual relationships which we ask of

our heterosexual ordinands. We recommend this because we consider the opening of the ordination process to gays and lesbians a matter of justice when justice should no longer be denied. . . . Explicitly opening the ordination process in this way is desirable to clear the Church of the taint of hypocrisy, since the presence of gay men and lesbians among the clergy is no secret. It may also be necessary if the Church is to counteract the irrational fear and hatred of gay men and lesbians rampant in our society; we cannot effectively advocate civil rights for gay men and lesbians in society at large if we appear to deny such rights within our fellowship.

Beyond these recommendations, the Commission reiterated the need for dialogue and the need for the Church to continue to inform itself on gay and lesbian issues.

Summary

After this review, one may still ask where the Episcopal Church stands on the two issues around which most of the debate has centered, namely, the blessing of same-sex unions and the ordination of noncelibate homosexuals.

In 1976, the General Convention affirmed the "equal claim of gay persons with all others to the care and pastoral concern of the Church." The House of Bishops, however, meeting in Port St. Lucie the following year, accepted a report declaring that neither blessing same-sex unions nor the ordination of noncelibate homosexual persons was appropriate. The 1979 Convention reaffirmed the Church's traditional teaching on marriage and sexual chastity and passed a resolution declaring the "inappropriateness" of ordaining noncelibate homosexuals. That resolution was ultimately dissented from by 29 bishops, and some bishops have acted contrary to it, taking it to be purely recommendatory and otherwise lacking the force of canon. Even in the face of these ordinations, the Church has never clarified the authority of that resolution.

The 70th General Convention

The last several Conventions have called for dialogue on the whole issue of sexuality, with the 70th Convention specifically acknowledging a discontinuity between the Church's teaching and the experience of many of its members. The 70th Convention also directed the House of Bishops to prepare a Pastoral Teaching on the matter, the aim of which would be to promote dialogue and provide direction. This document was to be produced prior to the 71st Convention in 1994.

The action of the 70th General Convention in Phoenix was an attempt to give a pastoral response to the issues and questions that had been raised. The Convention's action reflected that the Judeo-Christian understanding of humankind's relationship with God cannot be neatly packaged and easily handed on, but that understanding develops through prayer, Scripture study, worship, life in a community, mission, and in confrontation with the realities of history. Such realities of history include the many critical questions Church and synagogue have had to face at other historical crossroads. In reality, theology is generally done in response to questions raised either inside or outside the community of believers that come to challenge the current understanding of the faith.

The Jerusalem Church early faced the issue of whether and how to overcome the religious barrier between Jew and Gentile (non-Jew) so that the latter might be admitted to the Christian community without first being circumcised. Instead, by requiring abstention from sexual immorality and enforcing rules concerning food and its preparation in order to enable Jews and Gentiles to sit at the table and share a meal together, the early Church created an identity for itself which was neither Jew nor Gentile but Christian, an identity which called people together rather than separating them. This was an accommodation on both sides for the sake of community.

The critical questioning of history tests the limits of understanding. Galileo's and then Darwin's theories forced the Church to review and revise the theological understanding of their time about the nature of the world. They required serious and painful adjustments which in some ways we are still working through. Today's questions are also often painful and raise issues with which the Church would rather not deal. Many today would rather not face the challenge to the Church's traditional interpretation of Scripture raised by questions about human sexuality. Some would even say these are not legitimate questions. What is clear is that challenges are not new, that the function of theology is to grapple with such challenges, and that the questions being asked of the Church today, like some of those of yesterday, may result in new insights and a deeper and more comprehending faith.

So, the questions raised by history present challenges and challenges require a response. In Phoenix, the General Convention responded in a thoroughly Anglican way. A clearly received principle from deep within the tradition was affirmed. The historical challenge to that principle was acknowledged. And a pastoral response was formulated—Resolution A104sa concerning human sexuality:

> *Resolved,* the House of Deputies concurring, That the 70th General Convention of the Episcopal Church affirms that the teaching of the Episcopal Church is that physical sexual expression is appropriate only within the lifelong monogamous "union of husband and wife

in heart, body, and mind intended by God for their mutual joy; for the help and comfort given one another in prosperity and adversity and, when it is God's will, for the procreation of children and their nurture in the knowledge and love of the Lord" as set forth in the Book of Common Prayer; and be it further

Resolved, That this Church continue to work to reconcile the discontinuity between this teaching and the experience of many members of this body; and be it further

Resolved, That this General Convention confesses our failure to lead and to resolve this discontinuity through legislative efforts based upon resolutions directed at singular and various aspects of these issues; and be it further

Resolved, That this General Convention commissions the Bishops and members of each Diocesan Deputation to initiate a means for all congregations in their jurisdiction to enter into dialogue and deepen their understanding of these complex issues; and further this General Convention directs the President of each Province to appoint one Bishop, one lay deputy, and one clerical deputy in that Province to facilitate the process, to receive reports from the dioceses at each meeting of their Provincial Synod and report to the 71st General Convention; and be it further

Resolved, That this General Convention directs the House of Bishops to prepare a Pastoral Teaching prior to the 71st General Convention using learnings from the diocesan and provincial processes and calling upon such insight as is necessary from theologians, theological ethicists, social scientists, and gay and lesbian persons; and that three lay persons and three members of the clergy from the House of Deputies, appointed by the President of the House of Deputies, be included in the preparation of the Pastoral Teaching.

The resolution thus affirmed the principle that "the teaching of the Episcopal Church is that physical sexual expression is appropriate only within the lifelong, monogamous union [of marriage] as set forth in the Book of Common Prayer." In the context of Bible study, Eucharist, prayer, and sometimes painfully honest debate, the majority of bishops and deputies clearly upheld that this Prayer Book teaching is part of the received Judeo-Christian tradition of the Church.

These same bishops and deputies also recognized the historical reality—"the discontinuity between this teaching and the experience of many members [of the Church]"—that the way some followers of Jesus live constitutes a challenge to the traditional teaching. The Convention declared its resolve to "continue to work to reconcile" this discontinuity. It must be said here that taking time to reconcile the discontinuity of practice with the teachings of sacred Scripture and the received tradition of the Church is not new. Christians have yet to reconcile and resolve the conflict that exists between the clear ethical teaching of Jesus from the Sermon on the Mount in Matthew's gospel and the practice of most of us concerning, for instance, war ("Love your enemies and pray for those who persecute you"), or the pursuit of wealth ("Do not store up for yourselves treasures on earth where moths and woodworms destroy them and thieves break in and steal").

Members of the Church seem to live rather comfortably with the discontinuity of our material wealth—having a choice about tonight's dinner, having access to an automobile or public transportation, having more than one pair of shoes or a change of underwear—and the way 90% of the people in this world live. We expect interest on our savings accounts and our investments, despite the scriptural prohibitions respecting money and interest.

And perhaps the most obvious discontinuity we currently live with in the area of sexual relationships is the practice of divorce and remarriage which stands in the face of Jesus's explicit prohibition against both the dissolution of and the contracting of subsequent marriages found in the synoptic gospels, in particular, Mark 10:2–9. As a Church, we believe addressing the latter discontinuity, for instance, in the manner in which we have, on balance, has resulted in a more faithful Church, given all the factors that may be involved. (Data from those who participated in the dialogues on human sexuality generated by Resolution A104sa of the 1991 General Convention indicate that among 15,342 respondents, 8.5% are divorced and 13% are divorced and remarried.) In the case of other of the discontinuities cited, instead of honestly struggling to resolve them, we have forgotten that they are discontinuities with Scripture at all. Just as sustaining challenges to current understandings of the faith is not novel and not necessarily a bad thing, neither is struggling with discontinuity novel or without value.

While pledging itself to reconciliation of the discontinuity between the Church's traditional teaching on marriage and the experience of many of its members, the Convention recognized that legislation is not the appropriate way to deal with issues of human intimacy and that therefore it must acknowledge its inability "to lead and to resolve this discontinuity through legislative efforts based upon resolutions directed at singular and various aspects of these issues." The gospel, the Convention thus said, cannot be lived by law. If it is to become alive, it must first be lived with human responsibility and divine empowerment. So, having affirmed the principle (the received tradition), having recognized the practice (the experience of many members), the Convention then considered what the pastoral response should be.

Finally, the resolution commissioned each Bishop and members of each diocesan deputation "to initiate a means for all congregations to enter into dialogue and deepen their understanding of these complex issues" and directed the House of Bishops "to prepare a Pastoral Teaching prior to the 71st General Convention using the learnings from the diocesan and provincial processes and calling upon such insight as is necessary from theologians, theological ethicists, social scientists, and gay and lesbian persons."

Clearly, it was felt that the Church needed more time to be able to speak the truth in love, recognizing that for many, if not for most, change will not be possible unless they see how Scripture and tradition can be faithfully interpreted to support a new position. The resolution admitted that we needed time to make honest witness and testimony to one another and to trust that, in the context of prayer and mission, the Holy Spirit would lead the Church to the right place. Since the Church is basically a community of witness, it seemed necessary to take the risk of allowing people to tell their stories. Such stories need to be told in the context of "baptismal discourse," where Christians gather to speak to one another about the implications of the Baptismal Covenant. This process must begin with prayerful consideration of the Baptismal Creed and the five promises contained in the Baptismal Covenant (BCP, pp. 304-305), one of which is a promise to "strive for justice and peace among all people, and respect the dignity of every human being."

Baptismal discourse confronts compromises that suggest that Christians have to live "in the real world." Baptismal discourse lifts up how Christians have chosen to perceive reality and affirms that the "really real world" has been disclosed in Jesus Christ. Reality is what God is doing in Jesus Christ, and

15

that reality has to do with living in community today in ways that preview tomorrow's Kingdom of God.

"Let us dream of a Church," Presiding Bishop Edmond Browning said at Phoenix, "that refuses to settle its disputes and divisions by legislation, that refuses to accomplish with law what only the gospel can do." And former Archbishop of Canterbury, the Most Reverend Robert Runcie, speaking at the concluding Convention Eucharist, invited the Episcopal Church to consider that the Holy Spirit "leads us into all truth, as in everything else, through relationship, by staying in discourse with those whose views may appall us, without rubbishing their spiritual integrity."

"The Spirit of Truth," he continued, "is also the Spirit of Love, the one who rescues faith from being turned into the poison of bigotry. What I long for in your Church and mine [is] that we shall presume our opponents' reasoning has something to do with his or her desire to be loyal to the same Christ we want to serve ourselves [and that] we shall recognize that what is and is not a matter of fundamental loyalty to Christ cannot always be made clear in a generation."

---

[1] A brief report on these dialogues will be found in the Appendix to this Pastoral Study Document.

[2] In fact, the ordinal for bishops enjoins them to be a wholesome example "for the entire flock of Christ" (BCP, p. 517); the ordinal for priests specifies "to your people" (BCP, p. 532); it is only the ordinal for deacons that uses the form "to all people" (BCP, p. 544).

[3] A minority report dissenting from the conclusions of the majority was also filed.

2
DIALOGUE IN COMMUNITY

Communion in Faith

Since the 70th General Convention in 1991, some in our Church have participated in the dialogues on human sexuality mandated by Resolution A104sa. From the perspective of proportionality, the number of participants (approximately 18,000) was not large, but it was very significant. The survey forms filled out by the participants, while not intended to be a plebiscite or referendum on these critical issues, will contribute substantially to the ongoing conversation on human sexuality in our faith community. It is our considered opinion that the dialogues should continue, for, at this time, these are not matters which can be settled by a poll or by voting resolutions.

The Church's greatest resource in addressing the complex issues are committed communities of Christians where concerns can be addressed in open dialogue, in a setting that feels secure. Our greatest resource then is tied to the strength of our communion with each other—a communion created and sustained by the Holy Spirit.

The realization of the truth of God's revelation came to the disciples as pure gift. On the night before his death, Jesus promised the disciples that he would intercede with the Father to send "another Paraclete" who would always remain with the community. Communion with God will come as a gift of the Holy Spirit, the Paraclete, the Spirit of truth. The Holy Spirit will bear witness to the teaching and life of Jesus. The Holy Spirit will "prove the world wrong about sin and righteousness and judgment: about sin, because they do not believe" in Jesus

(John 16:8). The Spirit of God will be the presence of God truthfully telling the disciples of Christ; it will be the revelation of God the Father and God the Son (John 14:17; 15:26, 27; 16:13). By the power of the Holy Spirit a communion of disciples is formed, a Church is founded that will describe itself historically as "the temple of God" (1 Cor. 3:16), "a chosen race, a royal priesthood, a holy nation, God's own people" (1 Peter 2:9), the Body of Christ (1 Cor. 12:27).

These images of self-definition from the Apostolic period speak deeply of a holy communion with God: Father, Son, and Holy Spirit. Anglicans understand that this communion *(koinonia)* determines theologically our relationship with one another in the Church. *Koinonia* is the property or state of having something or someone in common. What is said to be held in common is not specified by the word *koinonia*. If we are to talk about our communion with one another, we must therefore also be clear about what it is we have in common. For example, intimacy and friendship, of necessity, are about something— they are rooted in something shared, something held in common. Knowing this, the author of the First Epistle of John writes to share his experience of Christ: "That which we have seen and heard we proclaim also to you, so that you may have fellowship *[koinonia]* with us; and our fellowship *[koinonia]* is with the Father and with his son Jesus Christ" (1 John 1:3). In the same way, our communion is about having something in common, sharing something in friendship and intimacy—our faith in Jesus Christ.

Communion with God and one another is both gift and divine expectation for the Church. The Church is that community in the world which is already open to receiving the love of God and to being enfolded into the orbit of God's life. Awareness of this reality moves St. Paul to address the Corinthian community, the most divided of all communities in the early Church, in these words: "To the church of God that is in Corinth, to those who are sanctified in Christ Jesus, called to be saints, together with all those who in every place call on the name of our Lord Jesus Christ, both their Lord and ours" (1 Cor. 1:2).

In baptism, by the gift and power of the Holy Spirit, Christians die with Christ and rise to the new life. Thus the baptized are united to God, the Holy Trinity, and brought into a relationship of holy communion with all the baptized through the ages, the Communion of Saints. The Church's response to and experience of the gift of *koinonia,* holy communion, is in fact the matter of the spiritual life.

The experience of communion is at once personal and corporate and is linked to liturgy and mission. The daily discipline and practice of liturgical and private prayer, the nurture of biblical teaching and meditation, the celebration of word and sacrament, the shared life of love and pastoral care, a passion for justice and peace, are the essential elements of the spiritual life that provide the necessary environment for the people of God to experience *koinonia,* holy communion with God and one another in the Body of Christ.

The Baptismal Covenant

Sometimes controversies over difficult issues make it easy to forget the real depth of our communion in faith. Polarization can lead us to believe that those things which might divide us are greater than what unites us, the basis of our communion. Yet, as we read in our quote from John's First Epistle, our communion is rooted by faith in the proclamation of the mystery of Christ which also unites us into the *koinonia* of the Triune God. We find this basis of our communion within the Church clearly set forth in the baptismal covenant:

Do you believe in God the Father?
I believe in God, the Father almighty, creator of heaven and earth.

Do you believe in Jesus Christ, the Son of God?
I believe in Jesus Christ, his only Son, our Lord.
>He was conceived by the power of the Holy Spirit and born of the Virgin Mary.
>He suffered under Pontius Pilate, was crucified, died, and was buried.
>He descended to the dead.
>On the third day he rose again.
>He ascended into heaven, and is seated at the right hand of the Father.
>He will come again to judge the living and the dead.

Do you believe in God the Holy Spirit?
>I believe in the Holy Spirit,
>>the holy catholic Church,
>>the communion of saints,
>>the forgiveness of sins,
>>the resurrection of the body,
>>and the life everlasting.

Will you continue in the apostles' teaching and fellowship, in the breaking of bread, and in the prayers?
I will, with God's help.

Will you persevere in resisting evil, and, whenever you fall into sin, repent and return to the Lord?
I will, with God's help.

*Will you proclaim by word and example the Good
News of God in Christ?*
I will, with God's help.

*Will you seek and serve Christ in all persons, loving
your neighbor as yourself?*
I will, with God's help.

*Will you strive for justice and peace among all
people, and respect the dignity of every human being?*
I will, with God's help.

Because of this faith covenant, we can believe that that which
unites us in communion is far greater than any issue or contro-
versy over which our membership has disagreement. We do not
need to fall victim to the false belief that true unity only exists
where everyone agrees on everything. We are a diverse Church
with a variety of perspectives and opinions. Such diversity can
be advantageous as we wrestle with complex issues. Further,
our ability to live with ambiguity without being driven to settle
questions prematurely is not only a sign of maturity but is also
a measure of our security in faith. These are strengths, not weak-
nesses. These strengths and our communion in one baptism are
also the means by which we can, with the leading of the Holy
Spirit, find solutions to the many concerns which confront the
Church. This was most clearly stated in the report of the Sec-
tion on Dogmatic and Pastoral Concerns of the Lambeth Conference of 1988:

Communion with Christ also means communion
with all those who belong to Christ. Through the
response of faith and of baptism, Christians enter a living
Body, the Church, of persons committed to relationship
with one another. In the New Testament the implications

of this are spelt out realistically and concretely. It implies the task of the overcoming of divisions imposed by culture, whether of race, class or caste, or sexual discrimination (Gal. 3:28, "You are all one in Christ Jesus"). It means giving material help to those in need (Rom. 15:27). It means esteeming each and every believer for the gift which the Holy Spirit has bestowed, to be used for the benefit of the whole body (1 Cor. 12:13-30). Thus the Gospel establishes as the normative pattern of the life of the community a relationship of interdependence, a mutuality between persons.

As we move ahead in our ongoing dialogues on human sexuality let us hold fast to the communion we share. Seeking always to realize the fullest possibilities of the communion given to us in the one baptism we share, we will not allow disagreement about any issue that is not a central affirmation of our Christian faith to disrupt our communion.

Having such a rule of faith means our communities are built on the strongest foundation. Having such a rule of faith means dialogues which take place in such communities will be open and honest—and the participants will have a sense of security. It is in such settings that the Holy Spirit can lead.

3
THE BIBLE AND HUMAN SEXUALITY

The Bible is a collection of sacred scriptures composed over a 1200-year period. It is made up of a variety of types of writings. Much of it is in stories, reflections on human circumstances and conditions in which God is frequently seen to be directly or indirectly involved. Often the voices heard in the Bible indicate that they are engaged in interpretation, seeking to understand and make relevant and pertinent for their time the traditions and experiences given to them.

These traditions are often about struggle—between order and chaos, freedom and slavery, justice and injustice, life and death. Amid suffering and evil, they tell of hope and the victories of the power of God's righteousness and love, especially in the resurrection of Jesus. Above all, the Bible is about God's love and concern for God's people.

While there have always been different emphases with regard to an understanding of the inspiration of the Scriptures, the catechism of the Book of Common Prayer (p. 853) states the essential Anglican and catholic view. Scriptures are called "the Word of God because God inspired their human authors and because God still speaks to us through the Bible." On the one hand, the Bible is fully an historical book. An analogy can be made with the Incarnation. Jesus was fully a human being. "He had to become like his brothers and sisters in every respect . . ." (Heb. 2:17). Yet we believe God was mysteriously and wondrously present in this circumscribed life. The Bible, then, is an historical book. Its viewpoint is regularly limited by the understandings and even prejudices of its time. And, we also believe, God spoke through these very circumstances and continues to speak to us today. We call Scriptures the Word of God because we may hear God's Spirit speaking to us through the Bible, but the Bible functions as a kind of icon, pointing its hearers through its words to the Word of God—to the Divine—revealed particularly as the eternal, incarnate, and risen Word of God.

Interpreting the Scriptures

Anglican and catholic theology has always understood the importance and the necessity of interpreting the Scriptures. Although some passages may or may seem to speak more directly than others, there is still the task of setting them within the larger context of the entire biblical drama and revelation. In this sense, no one passage or verse can tell the whole story or be interpreted in isolation. What gives the Bible its ultimacy is its overarching narrative power for shaping our understanding of life and of God's purpose and character—its telling of how God's reign can be already present in a world which often seems inchoate and broken.

The tradition of the Church, together with human reason reflecting on experience, are the means of interpretation. Tradition is a word used several ways in the Church, with different levels of authority.[1] The Tradition (capital T) is the risen, living Jesus Christ, our Lord and Savior. The process of tradition is the natural mechanism through which the Spirit of God works in every place and in every age of the history of the Church, the process by which the faith is transmitted from generation to generation and from culture to culture. In recent years women and others, whose predecessors might at first not seem to have played that great a role in the Bible or tradition, have helped bring a hearing of other voices within the Bible and tradition. They have brought new perspectives and insights. The traditions (lower case and plural) of the Church are our fallible human attempts to express the living Tradition, in response to the urgings of the Holy Spirit in our faith community, in different times and places and cultures.

Reason has provided the means by which we express and communicate God's revelation. Reason is the divinely implanted faculty for receiving the divine revelation. Reason, however, is much more than logical analysis. It is best understood as prayerful, rational reflection on the Scriptures in the light of human experience and sound learning; it is also prayerful, rational reflection on human experience and sound learning in the light of the Scriptures. Reason is one means by which the Holy Spirit works to enable us to discern the mind and will of God in our day. Reason is not a distinct source of knowledge unrelated to the Scriptures, nor is reason infallible.

The Bible may regularly be used to critique tradition and reason, but it never can be heard without them. It is not a matter of whether we will use them to be part of the conversation with the Scriptures. They are always present. The important question is whether we will use them in a conscious, mature, and prayerful way.

The biblical writings were formed in communities. While individuals can read and study the Bible for themselves, and so be edified and spiritually nourished, it is through the hearing of and reflection upon the Bible in communities of faith that the Bible has its most important role in convicting, guiding, inspiring. The Spirit takes what is of Jesus, "declaring it to you," and, indeed, brings deeper understanding of truth (John 16:12–15).

The Scriptures themselves contain many voices and perspectives. It is often pointed out that the four Gospels give us a much richer view of Jesus because of their differences. This diversity is true of all of the Bible. Religious practices and even many beliefs vary and change from the time of a wandering desert tribe to the era of temple worship, through exile and return, with emphases on kingship, prophecy, priesthood, and wisdom teaching. Even in the New Testament, written over a much shorter period of time, we find that the church for whom the Gospel of John was written was quite different from those churches out of which the Gospel of Matthew emerged, and that the church of Corinth was clearly quite different than the one to which the Letter to the Hebrews was written.

What gives the Bible its unity throughout all these changes and variations is its constantly recurring and passionate call to worship the one and only God, the holy God who is both demanding of justice and righteousness while full of compassion and mercy. This God calls the people of God to "be holy, for I the Lord your God am holy" (Lev. 19:2). The calling to follow the ways of God and to know God's holiness comes for Christians to its fullness through the life, death, and risen life of Jesus.

Human Sexuality in the Scriptures

It is not, then, surprising that the biblical views about sexuality are thoroughly enmeshed in cultural and historical circumstances and describe some considerable diversity of practice. Polygamy, for example, is not only known but at times presented as quite acceptable. Women and children are virtually or actually treated as property in highly patriarchal cultures (although patriarchy seems to be viewed as the result of sin in Genesis 3:16). Sexual mores are governed or influenced by various taboos and concerns about ritual purity which are believed to be important, sometimes for health reasons, and also in order not to confuse lines of inheritance and the bloodlines of clan and group. Procreation and the continuation of the people are, understandably, important concerns.

Numerous biblical stories reveal a quite straightforward and realistic view of sexuality. It is a powerful human drive which can lead to sin and even disaster for individuals and the community. Although the view of sexuality as bordering on the sinful, which came later to play a strong role in some Christian traditions, is not a significant part of the Bible, there is certainly the recognition that sexual practice needs to be restrained and controlled to be beneficial. Sexuality is, therefore, always a matter of concern for the community and never a matter just of individual choice or behavior or of concern only to a man and a woman. In this context the nurture and right upraising and teaching of children are a primary interest in which both mothers and fathers are seen to have important roles.

From the beginning—from the early chapters of Genesis onward—there is also a sense of mystery and awe that "male and female God created them" (Gen.1:27). There is not only the marvel of being able to share in the process of bringing new life to the world, but the wonder of the two who are different joining together. Jesus speaks of this wonder when he says, "For this reason a man shall leave his father and mother and be joined to his wife, and the two shall become one flesh. So they are no longer two but one flesh" (see Mark 10:7–8 and Gen. 2:24).

Never viewed apart from human animality, sexual behavior also gains a purposefulness and character which, with all else that is human, takes on a potential for self-giving love and beauty. The Song of Songs celebrates its erotic aspects, and there develops in the New Testament a strong sense of the sanctity of marriage and its solemnity and mutuality. Although not fully emergent from its patriarchal acculturation, the view of marriage and the Christian household found in the Letter to the Ephesians (5:21—6:4) describes both a tenderness and a self-giving love that shares in Christ's way of loving.

It is, however, Jesus himself who moves both the solemnity and mutuality of marriage to a new level in his teaching about divorce (see Mark 10:2–12; Luke 16:18; Matt. 5:31–32, 19:3–9). He is clearly critical of the earlier biblical teaching. It is "because of your hardness of heart that Moses wrote this commandment . . . allowing a man to write a certificate of dismissal and divorce his wife" (see Deut. 24:1–4). Instead Jesus emphasized that the two became one flesh. "Therefore, what God has joined together, let no one separate." Men, in other words, are not to divorce their wives, leaving them in many ways helpless in such male-dominated society. Whoever does this, Jesus said, commits adultery against his wife when he marries another woman, and also makes his former wife an adulteress, should she be forced to join herself to another man as the only way to find support and protection.

While it would be hard to weaken the solemnity with which Jesus evidently viewed the marriage covenant, Jesus elsewhere teaches about forgiveness and new beginnings. His remarkable (astounding for his time) acceptance of women into his company and ministry suggests that his prophetic attitude toward women and his concern with male indifference and cruelty were paramount in his teaching on divorce. Similarly his sharp saying, " . . . that everyone who looks at a woman with lust has already committed adultery with her in his heart" (Matt. 5:28), seems intended to challenge his male followers to control their sexuality and so not need to inhibit the lives of women in order to protect men from their own lusts.

The biblical books occasionally consider other forms of sexual behavior along with abstinence. Eunuchs, either from birth or due to castration, are heard of from time to time. Celibacy is recognized as a proper vocation for those called to it, strong friendships are exemplified, and a chaste life is held up for all. While adultery is the worse sin because of what it does to the marriage covenant and community, fornication is also disapproved of, especially when it is linked to a general kind of licentiousness often associated with the Gentile world. It was seen to show a lack of seriousness about the community, about the vocation of marriage, and the care of progeny. Prostitution is known and particularly condemned in connection with false and idolatrous worship of other gods. A view of purity, on the other hand, is upheld—one which sees sexuality as good when it is used and enjoyed for the procreation of children, the benefit of the covenant of marriage, and the strengthening of the community.

Homosexuality in the Scriptures

We now turn to seven specific passages in Scripture which refer to homosexual practice. In doing so, we recognize the danger inherent in isolating specific texts and acknowledge that we must look to the witness of Scripture as a whole. We also acknowledge that there is significant disagreement among us as to how Scripture is to be used and interpreted as we seek to apply it to this complex subject.

Genesis 19:1-29

Interpreters will disagree about the "sin of Sodom." Some hold that the offense of Sodom is to be understood with specific reference to sexuality, others that the offense centers on the theme of hospitality. But even if the story centers on hospitality, there are those who contend that the homosexuality issue clearly lies behind it and is not excluded by it. The force of the word "know" (*yada*) cannot be overlooked so that the sexual element is removed. The offense against hospitality is so starkly evil precisely because it involves sexual behavior which is taken for granted to be wrong. The violent aspect of the gang-rape of guests is the issue, and Lot attempts to protect his guests by making the atrocious offer of his virgin daughters to the men of Sodom. The parallel story in Judges 19-20 tells of a Levite who was a guest in Gibeah. The men of the city wanted to have intercourse with him, so his host offers his virgin daughter and his guest's concubine as substitutes. The men of the city rape and kill the concubine. Chapter 20 recounts the vengeance taken on the men of Gibeah for their actions. In both cases, the proposed rape of the guest and the rape of the concubine is called vile —a "vile thing" (19:23, 24) and a "vile outrage" (20:6). We cannot claim it is this evil or that: it clearly is both, with the sexual fault making more blatant the wrong of inhospitality.

But many interpreters point out that the story of Sodom is of little help in our contemporary discussion of homosexuality, since the moral debate today revolves around lifelong, committed, and stable relationships between people of the same sex. The intent of the men of Sodom to humiliate Lot's guests, who were angels sent by God in the appearance of men, by gang-raping them would presumably be condemned by everyone.

There are those who would argue that the "sin of Sodom" is not specifically a sexual sin but a general disorder of society. Ezekiel 16:49-50 understands the evil of Sodom to be pride, greed, and neglect of the poor, as does Isaiah 1:9-31. In Isaiah 3:9 the reference is to injustice, and in Jeremiah 23:14 the prophets have become like the inhabitants of Sodom and Gomorra: "they commit adultery and walk in lies; they strengthen the hands of evil doers, so that no one turns from wickedness." Here as elsewhere, homosexuality is not raised as an issue. Jesus, when referring to the mistreatment of his own disciples, seems to stand in a line of interpretation which views the sin of Sodom as inhospitality (Luke 10: 10-12; Matt. 10:14-15; see Luke 17:29 and Matt. 11:23-24). However, while the disorder is a general one, human sexuality is one of the specific manifestations of that disorder and cannot be discounted.

Leviticus 18:22 and 20:13

The Holiness Code in Leviticus explicitly prohibits male homosexual intercourse: "You shall not lie with a male as with a woman; it is an abomination" (Lev. 18:22). In Leviticus 20:10-16 the same act is listed as one of a series of sexual offenses—along with adultery, incest, and bestiality—that are punishable by death.

Some point out that these passages occur in a context of teaching about ritual and moral holiness, a number of which would not seem applicable to life today. Readers are told, for instance, that it is an abomination to sow fields with two kinds of seed or to put on a garment made of two different materials (Lev. 19:19). Menstruation is seen as a sickness, and if a man and a woman have intercourse during this period, both of them are to be cut off from the people (Lev. 20:18). A man maimed or deformed in any way cannot be ordained as a priest (21:18-21), and pork and seafood without fins and scales must not be eaten (Lev. 11:7, 10-11). There are those who remind us that although it is always good to pay close attention to wisdom from the past (and Christians continue to follow a number of teachings from the *torah* of the Hebrew Scriptures), many of the understandings of earlier peoples about purity, order, and sex having to do with property rights, are quite different from our own. When, led by the Holy Spirit, Paul and Peter turned from the exclusiveness of the Levitical code and accepted Gentiles into the Church, the message of Christianity took on new power and invitation.

Others put more weight on the authority of the moral codes of the Hebrew Scriptures. They point out that as Jesus criticized food laws but upheld the Ten Commandments, mainstream Christianity has always recognized the authority of the ethical commands of the Old Testament. Thus, the Thirty-nine Articles of Religion lay down that while Christians are not bound by the ceremonial, ritual, and civil laws of the Old Testament, no one is free from the commandments which are called "moral" (Article 7).

That part of Leviticus which has as its theme the necessity for Israel to be holy because the Lord who is in the midst of them is holy mixes together a wide variety of commands: dietary regulations or laws against occult practices appear alongside rules for honesty in commerce or injunctions to honor the elderly and to love as yourself even the foreigner who lives in your community. The fact is that the Old Testament does not make distinctions between moral goodness and ritual purity in the way the New Testament does. Yet portions of the Holiness Code were used in the catechetical instruction preserved in some Pauline epistles and in 1 Peter.

However, there are those who question not only the appropriateness of the ritual regulations of the Hebrew Scriptures for Christians but, since ritual and moral codes are woven into one fabric, they also question the application of some aspects of the moral code, e.g., punishing those guilty of incest, adultery, and homosexual acts by being put to death.

An anthropological argument for this biblical prohibition against homosexual activity has to do with ensuring offspring. This prohibition, especially for males, is based on the assumption among ancients that all potential human life is contained in the semen. In this view, the woman is merely the receptacle. Where the viability and continuity of the tribe is at stake, any wasting of the semen—having sex with a menstruating woman, bestiality, masturbation, or homosexual activity—which precluded procreation is forbidden.

From a theological perspective, the climactic handiwork of God was in the creation of male and female "in the image of God" (Gen. 1:27). God's command and blessing is, "Be fruitful and multiply, and fill the earth." Any activity on the part of males to thwart this command is seen as contrary to God's creative purposes.

Romans 1:18-32

The most significant passage is Romans 1:18-32, in which Paul views male homosexual behavior—and perhaps female as well—as more evidence of the moral depravity which has befallen Gentiles as punishment for their idolatry. Paul's warning in this passage is not that wrongful practice leads to false worship, but that false worship leads to wrongful behavior. The main concern is with wrong worship, a concern central to the whole biblical witness. Worshipping any god other than the holy God of righteousness would lead people astray. As a result, "God gave them up to dishonorable passions." There are two meanings of the Greek word for "gave up" *(paredoken)*. One translation is that "God abandoned them," i.e., God stood back and let the false worshippers have their own way. As a result, freedom is not grace at all but self-imposed bondage. The other translation for *paredoken* is "God delivered them over." The consequences, the "dishonorable passions," are imposed by God as a punishment. For Paul, the fundamental human sin is the refusal to honor God and give God thanks (1:21); consequently, God's wrath takes the form of letting human idolatry run its own self-destructive course. Homosexual behavior, then, is not a *provocation* of "the wrath of God" (Rom. 1:18); rather, it is a *consequence* of God's decision either to "give up" on his rebellious creatures or to "hand them over" to their own passions.

But just as Paul has his readers reveling in indignation at

the behavior of some, he reminds them of other kinds of wickedness, evil, covetousness, and malice. There is envy, murder, strife, deceit, craftiness, gossip, slander, insolence, God-hating, haughtiness, boastfulness, rebelliousness toward parents, foolishness, faithlessness, heartlessness, ruthlessness. And so, as the second chapter of Romans begins, he administers the final *coup de grace*: "... you have no excuse, whoever you are, when you judge others; for in passing judgment on another you condemn yourself, because you, the judge, are doing the very same things." In fact, no one can boast. All are called to repentance. That is the point. "There is no one who is righteous, not even one" (Rom. 3:10).

Some interpreters point out that Paul focuses on women exchanging natural intercourse for unnatural (the only reference to lesbian sexual behavior in the Bible), and men giving up natural intercourse with women (Rom. 1:26-27) because it is a particularly graphic image of the way in which the fallen state of humanity distorts God's created order. God the creator made man and woman for each other, to cleave together, to be fruitful and multiply. In Paul's view, when human beings engage in homosexual activity they enact an outward and visible sign of an inward and spiritual reality: the rejection of the Creator's design. They embody the spiritual condition of those who have "exchanged the truth about God for a lie."

Others, however, hold that Paul is talking here about heterosexuals who are committing homosexual acts. While it is unlikely that Paul knew of what we today call "homosexual or heterosexual orientation" (even the term "homosexual" was not coined until the nineteenth century), we must be careful not to minimize the main point of the text, which is God's judgment upon idolatry—and this extends to every area of human relationships.

1 Corinthians 6:9 and 1 Timothy 1:10

The early Church did, in fact, consistently adopt the Old Testament's teaching on the matters of sexual morality and on homosexual acts in particular. In 1 Corinthians 6:9 and 1 Timothy 1:10, we find persons who commit homosexual acts in lists of persons who do things unacceptable to God.

In 1 Corinthians 6, Paul, exasperated with the Corinthians— some of whom apparently believe themselves to have entered a spiritually exalted state in which moral rules no longer apply— confronts them with a blunt rhetorical question: "Do you not know that wrongdoers will not inherit the kingdom of God?" He then gives an illustrative list of the sorts of persons he means "fornicators, idolaters, adulterers"—and for the next two words we have no precise translation—"effeminate, abusers of themselves with mankind" (KJV) or "sexual perverts" (RSV) or "male prostitutes, sodomites" (NRSV). The words in the Greek original are *malakoi* and *arsenokoitai,* and herein is the problem and the debate.

The word *malakoi* is not a technical term meaning "homosexuals," for no such term existed either in Greek or Hebrew, but it appears often in Hellenistic Greek as pejorative slang to describe the "passive" partners—often young boys—in homosexual activity. In the Greek and Roman cultures it was not unusual for men to have a same-sex partner, usually a youth or an effeminate person. The word *malakoi* means "soft." The man was not looked down upon as long as he was not the passive partner. There was abroad in first and second century society a tendency to regard women as weaker, less rational, and inferior to men. As Peter Brown points out, a man "had to learn to exclude from his character and from the poise and temper of his body all telltale traces of 'softness' that might betray in him the half-formed state of a woman."[2] Some suggest that what Paul was talking about in these passages is pederasty, a common practice in the culture of his day, and in all likelihood prevalent in Corinth.

The rarely used word *arsenokoitai* may refer to a male prostitute at the service of either sex. The Hebrew word *mishkav zakur,* "lying with a male," in Leviticus 18:22 and 20:13 is translated in the Septuagint (Greek Old Testament) as *arsenos koiten.* Paul's use of the term presupposes and reaffirms the Holiness Code's condemnation of homosexual acts. Paul, as a Jew, may have found homosexuality particularly foreign because it was more widely known in the Hellenistic world and because it often involved prostitution and pederasty

Mark 10:6-8

Perhaps the most significant passage for our discussion is when Jesus addresses the fundamental meaning of sexuality by appealing to Genesis 1 and 2: "But from the beginning of creation, 'God made them male and female. For this reason a man shall leave his father and mother and be joined to his wife, and the two shall become one flesh'" (Mark 10:6-8). Thus, heterosexual love is the normative expression of sexual love according to the testimony of Scripture. Yet, Jesus' own celibate life witnesses to the fact that while intimate sexual relationship is a wonderful gift from God, it is, as Jesus is presented in the gospels, not necessary in order to be fully human.

For some Christians, the biblical verses cited above are heard in the context of the larger Christian teaching about the primacy of agape love and the radical, inclusive character of the Christian community. They remember Jesus' reaching out to those whom many religious people of the time had difficulty accepting. They know how the Bible has been used to exclude people. For others, these verses remain decisive against all homosexual practice, or at least they raise questions of such weight that they believe Christians should not affirm even the most committed gay and lesbian relationships. They are also concerned that the authority of the Bible, as they understand it, be upheld against interpretations based on contemporary mores and understandings.

Conclusion

Throughout the Bible, sexuality is seen as an important aspect of being human and of being the people of God. Faithful living is all of a piece, and all human relations are meant to find their deepest value in the context of their response to God's love. "We love because God first loved us" (1 John 4:19). Sexuality is never to be considered apart from the call to worship the holy God of justice and compassion and to respond in community with lives of sacrificial giving, peacemaking, mercy, fairness, honesty without hypocrisy, kindness, purity, generosity, and courage. Clearly Jesus has strong expectations that those who followed him in responding to the in-breaking of God's reign would lead such disciplined and obedient lives—lives that did not just follow natural impulses, but were to be characterized by gracefulness. His disciples were and are to be a different kind of people.

---

[1] P. C. Rodger and Lukas Visher, eds., *The Fourth World Conference on Faith and Order (New York*: Association Press, 1964), pp. 50–61; "Tradition and Traditions," *Faith and Order Findings,* Faith and Order Paper No. 40 (Minneapolis, MN: Augsburg Publishing House).

[2] Peter Brown, *The Body and Society: Man, Woman, and Sexual Renunciation in Early Christianity* (New York: Columbia University Press, 1988), p. 11.

4
A TRADITIONAL CHRISTIAN UNDERSTANDING OF MARRIAGE

It is our purpose in chapter four of this document to present the traditional teaching of the Episcopal Church on human sexuality and marriage. Since all Church doctrine must be rooted and grounded in Holy Scripture, we will seek to discern in the Bible the foundations of our understanding today. We will also examine the tradition of the Episcopal Church as it is embodied in the Declaration of Intention from Canon I.18(e) and the Exhortation at the beginning of the marriage liturgy of the Book of Common Prayer.

The Witness of Tradition

The present tradition of the Episcopal Church on human sexuality and marriage is our expression, in doctrine and worship, of the mind of Christ as we perceive it today from our understanding of Holy Scripture, from our understanding of earlier traditions of the Church, and in reasonable acceptance of the best scientific knowledge of our day. Within this process of tradition, Holy Scripture bears a special authority and status.

As we strive to interpret the Scriptures in our day, we need to take seriously the Church's various interpretations throughout history, with special attention to the early Church fathers, the creeds, and the ecumenical councils. We also need to understand both the historical context of the biblical writers and of our present cultural situation through which we perceive and experience what the Christian life of faith means. And when we study and interpret Scriptures we need to be aware of our current situation, contemporary experience, modern biblical and theological scholarship, and the revelations of God's truth in other disciplines of human inquiry.

The Scriptures, however, do not speak plainly or unconditionally about all matters. The traditions of the Church, therefore, also supplement the Scriptures. They are alive and, therefore, always changing. These traditions are not a separate or independent source of authority, but are a record of the various and changing interpretations of Scripture and the establishment of truth in areas with which the Scriptures do not deal, so long as they are not contrary to the Scriptures. Further, they include, for Anglicans, bishops' pastorals, the actions of General Conventions and Lambeth Conferences, the canons of the Church, Catechisms, and documents such as the Articles of Religion.

Further, it includes the various editions of the Book of Common Prayer and the Church's authorized hymn books. All these are intended to inform us as we try to understand the Scriptures and to interpret their meaning for our day. But, of course, tradition is not self-evident and needs to be interpreted also. Further, while they too are always changing, traditions do provide us with the wisdom of the community over time and in continuity with the past.

The Witness of Scripture

The witness of the New Testament on human sexuality and marriage brings us the ideal of lifelong, monogamous, heterosexual union as God's intention for the development of women and men as sexual persons. Any sexual activity outside of marriage, is seen as sinful. Holy Scripture also recognizes that God calls some to celibacy for particular vocation and service.

These boundaries point toward an understanding of holiness which is fundamental to the Church's teaching on marriage and human sexuality, though some traditional boundaries are being challenged by today's realities. The present teaching of the Episcopal Church on human sexuality and marriage is our expression, in doctrine and worship, of the mind of Christ as we perceive it today from our understanding of Holy Scripture, from earlier traditions of the Church, and in reasonable expression of the scientific knowledge of this day.

It is our faith as Christians that all truth comes from the one God. Facts discovered by reason are only one dimension of this truth, as science seeks to explain what happens and how it happens. By its nature, science cannot discover the meaning and purpose of life. The *facts* of human sexuality and how it functions are areas for scientific exploration. The *meaning* of our sexuality may be known only in our relationship with God, and most completely in our relationship with the self-revelation of God in Christ. The Church looks first to Holy Scripture for the standard of this revelation, then to the traditions which we have attempted to express in terms compatible with reason, logic, and the best scientific knowledge available. Scripture, reason, tradition: three ways by which truth comes to us, but all truth is one in God.

A Story of Creation

The first chapter of Genesis contains a creation story which in its present form is a product of sixth-century Judaism, the period of the Babylonian exile and return. It affirms the goodness of all creation, including human sexuality, which is emphasized in this account: "...it was very good" (Gen. 1:31). Other aspects of sexuality presented here include creation in the image of God, the simultaneous creation of female and male, and the divine command for men and women to use their reproductive powers to increase in numbers, to fill the earth and subdue it, and to dominate the rest of creation.

The image of God in which we are made is not here defined. We assume it must mean other than physical similarity, and include powers of reflective and abstract thought and communication, the gift of freedom, and the moral responsibility it entails. Perhaps when we consider it in the light of Jesus' life and personality, the image of God may best be described as our capacity to know the love of God and to respond. Man and woman are created simultaneously in this image. Equality of the sexes is clearly implied, as well as complementarity. Female and male are of equal dignity. They are interdependent, for together they are a representative of the wholeness of the divine image. Here is the foundation for the emphasis upon the companionship of sexual union.

Having made them equal and interdependent, the Creator now commands the man and woman: "Be fruitful and multiply, and fill the earth and subdue it..." (Gen. 1:28a). Later we shall see that the command to procreate can be and was interpreted in ways destructive of human life and dignity and of earth's ecology. For now, however, let us explore the more positive aspects of the reproductive function of human sexuality.

Natural science has made clear to us the importance of sexual reproduction in the evolution of life on earth. Probably the Lord God could have created us in some other way. But the fact is that sexual reproduction is the way God has chosen to create all complex life-forms on earth. We are all creatures of sexual reproduction, both in our species and in our individual persons. Creation continues today, both on the biological and the personal level. The word "procreate" means literally "forth to create." Perhaps it is on the personal level that parents, through faith in God, can begin to appreciate the miracle in which they have been invited to participate. It is a miracle of the creation of a new human person. This is an experience both humbling and exalting, to hold a newborn child and to realize that only God can make such a wonderful being, but that God, through our sexuality, permits us to share in our Creator's act of creating. "Be fruitful and multiply...." It is a blessing.

An Older Creation Story

When a group of Pharisees asked Jesus his opinion on the Mosaic law permitting divorce, Jesus responded: "But from the beginning of creation, 'God made them male and female. For this reason a man shall leave his father and mother and be joined to his wife, and the two shall become one flesh.' So they are no longer two, but one flesh. Therefore what God has joined together let no one separate" (Mark 10:6-9). Jesus here quotes from the older of the biblical creation stories, found in the second and third chapters of Genesis. This account was written in its present form two or three centuries before the account in Genesis 1.

In this creation story, for the man *[adam]*, "there was not found a helper as his partner" (Gen. 2:20b). So God takes a rib from *adam* and from it creates woman. The man then says, "This at last is bone of my bones and flesh of my flesh; this one shall be called Woman *[ishshah]*, for out of Man *[ish]* this one was taken" (Gen. 2:23). Here *adam* is humankind, man in a generic sense which includes both female and male in one. From humankind the Lord draws forth the female *[ishshah]*, leaving the male *[ish]*. In this is found the biblical foundation and meaning of human sexuality and marriage in the Jewish tradition: "Therefore a man leaves his father and his mother and clings to his wife, and they become one flesh. And the man and his wife were both naked, and were not ashamed" (Gen. 2:24-25). Having been created from one flesh, in sexual union without shame woman and man again become one flesh. Companionship joins procreation as a God-given purpose for sexual intercourse. Marriage is endorsed by our Creator for the mutual re-creation of the wholeness of humankind, one flesh.

Realistically, the actual working of human sexuality in this world does not always reflect the goodness intended by our Creator. We live in a fallen world where sin distorts every part of God's creation, including our sexuality. Sexual abuse, exploitation, male dominance, rape, incest, pornography, prostitution, promiscuity, pedophilia—all are facts of life. The biblical explanation for these corruptions is called "evil imagination," the misuse of our God-given creativity to imagine and do that which is contrary to the will of God. Genesis expresses it this way: "The Lord saw that the wickedness of humankind was great in the earth, and that every inclination of the thoughts of their hearts was only evil continually" (Gen. 6:5). The story of Genesis 3 is a dramatization of this doctrine of evil imagination. Because humankind turns away from God, all of God's best gifts, including human sexuality, are corrupted. The pain of childbirth is attributed to the fall, yet woman's sexual desire continues to be for the man. The dominance of men over women is blamed on the fall: "…and he shall rule over you" (Gen. 3:16b). These twin biblical truths, the goodness of sexuality and of all God's creation, and the corruption of sexuality and of all God's creation, are both dealt with in many ways in Jewish and Christian traditions, in the Bible, and in history.

Some Jewish Traditions

Non-theological factors drove much of the development of the Jewish traditions of sexuality and marriage. The need for increase in population to compete with the neighboring nations made procreation far more important than companionship as a purpose for sexuality and marriage. In the early part of Israel's history, polygamy was accepted for those men able to afford more wives, so that they might produce more children. Slavery was accepted, and sexual relations between free men and female slaves were assumed and regulated. It was a male dominated society in which men alone had property rights, which included not only real property but extended to the lives and bodies of women and children as well. Divorce was a male prerogative, and female barrenness was a cause for divorce. Adultery, seduction, and rape were condemned as abrogations of the property rights of men.

The Song of Solomon is a folk song in praise of sexual love, celebrating youthful passion, with no reference to God or to marriage. Taking the form of a dialogue between a young woman and a young man in love with each other, this book probably had its origins in the early influence of the fertility cults of their neighbors upon Jewish culture and was then assumed into annual Jewish festivals and so into the Bible. It affirms that sexual love is in itself good and beautiful.

Just the opposite tendency can be seen in the later Holiness Code in Leviticus (Lev. 17-26). Here the priests of Israel were struggling to differentiate themselves from the sexually promiscuous practices of Canaanite religion. Incest, adultery, homosexual relations, sexual relations with animals, child sacrifice, resorting to mediums and wizards, sexual relations during a woman's menstrual period, and many other "abominations" are prohibited because these are the things the Canaanites do, for, "You shall not do as they do in the land of Egypt, where you lived, and you shall not do as they do in the land of Canaan, to which I am bringing you" (Lev. 18:3). For Christians, such practices must be judged not by their Canaanite connections, but by our understanding of the mind of Christ.

Jesus and the New Covenant

Jesus is not a reformer of Jewish sexual ethics. He is a revolutionary. His teaching calls for a radical cleansing of temple idols and a return to the foundations of God's intentions in creation. Jesus overturned the Mosaic divorce law, rejected men's prerogative to divorce at will, and asserted the will of the Creator: "But from the beginning of creation, 'God made them male and female. For this reason a man shall leave his father and mother and be joined to his wife, and the two shall become one flesh'" (Mark 10:6-8a). Companionship seems far too weak a synonym for this doctrine of "one flesh," the primary purpose intended by God for marriage and sexual union. The purpose of procreation, which predominated in both Jewish and Christian teaching, no longer stands alone.

Jesus rejects divorce absolutely. It may be a fact of life, but divorce can have no divine sanction in the teaching of Christ: "So they are no longer two, but one flesh. Therefore what God has joined together let no one separate" (Mark 10:8b-9). This teaching of Jesus is a call to radical new freedom in the reign of God. It is part of a new vision which had power to survive government persecutions and to prevail as the faith of the Empire. Elaine Pagels has observed, "By subordinating the obligation to procreate, rejecting divorce, and implicitly sanctioning monogamous relationships, Jesus reverses traditional priorities, declaring, in effect, that the other obligations, including marital ones, are now more important than procreation."[1]

If applied legalistically, this could be harsh, puritanical, unloving, inhuman ethic. But Jesus never uses it that way. Think, for example, of his gently dealing with the woman caught in the act of adultery, and with the Samaritan woman at the well, who had been married to five husbands and was living with one to whom she was not married. The Church, in producing the New Testament, remembered these as typical of Jesus' always upholding the absolute standard of the will of God, while gently accepting people as they are. It is an example for the Church to follow in both ethical teaching and in pastoral application.

Jesus then offered an even more radical teaching, going beyond the Jewish tradition exalting marriage and family above all else. Jesus told his disciples, "Not everyone can accept this teaching, but only those to whom it is given. For there are eunuchs who have been so from birth, and there are eunuchs for the sake of the kingdom of heaven. Let anyone accept this who can" (Matt. 19:11-12). Jesus does not prohibit marriage, and marriage is certainly not an impediment to entering the kingdom of heaven. Marriage and family and sexuality are all good, all gifts of God.[2] Jesus' own human life is our supreme example of a holy single life dedicated totally to God. Nothing in the world can be more important than that hidden treasure, that pearl of great price, the reign of God.

Paul, in those letters generally attributed to his authorship, gives practical advice to Christians which generally follows Jesus' radical teaching. In Romans 1, Paul believes homosexual conduct is the defilement of the body that God gave him, a body that is in some sense stamped with God's image. Paul felt strongly about all types of sexual sin, but regarded the homosexual lifestyle as far worse than simple fornication. This is a crucial teaching on homosexual behavior and is the basis for much of the received tradition. Homosexual behavior is one sign of creation falling away from God's intention for it. In his first letter to the Church in Corinth, Paul advises, "A man does well not to marry" (1 Cor. 7:1b). It seems better to him that everyone should follow his example and devote all his time and energy to the mission of Christ. "But because there is so much immorality, every man should have his own wife, and every woman should have her own husband" (1 Cor. 7:2). He forbids divorce on the part of Christians, but if an unbelieving spouse wishes to leave a Christian, so be it. Marriage is upheld as honorable, but the kingdom always comes first. Therefore Paul teaches it is better not to marry, but it is also better to marry than to "burn with passion" (1 Cor. 7:9). This view was certainly conditioned by Paul's belief in the imminent Second Coming. In contrast to the radical teachings of Jesus and Paul, the letter to the Ephesians (chapter 5) and the Pastoral Epistles return to extolling the virtues of the family, of companionship, and of procreation.

Post-Apostolic Developments

While the teachings of Jesus and Paul concerning marriage and thus human sexuality were in great measure shaped by their belief in the imminence of the kingdom of God, later generations saw the matter in a different light. For example, when the persecution of Christians came to an end at the beginning of the fourth century, and with it a virtual close to the list of martyrs, a new situation presented itself. As greater and greater numbers of people presented themselves for baptism there was a gradual lowering of Christian ideals and laxity in discipline that inevitably follows mass conversions.[3] This lowering of Christian ideals brought forth a new hero to replace the martyr—the ascetic.

The rise of monasticism coincided with the increased secularization of the Church brought on by the end of persecution and the establishment of Christianity as the state religion. In this context the ascetic replaced the martyr as the hero who gave up all for the sake of the kingdom of God. At the top of the list of those things included in this spiritual martyrdom was the maintaining of virginity and the valorization of celibacy. Thus the list of virgins joined the list of martyrs as the heroes of the Church.

We see then the gradual movement toward the recognition

of those leading lives without sexual activity as somehow living a higher or more perfect kind of Christian life. True asceticism meant living without sex. This asexual asceticism was eventually to have a major influence on the doctrine of Original Sin—the Fall. The scriptural basis for the development of the theology of Original Sin is found in the Pauline teaching that "sin came into the world through one man" so that "many died through the one man's trespass" (cf. Rom. 5:12–21).

This doctrine underwent further development in the late second century as the Church struggled against the dualistic heresies. But in the late fourth and early fifth centuries, under the influence of monastic asceticism, human sexual desire had become a primary focus of the Fall. While most writers on the subject believed that Adam and Eve had fallen from a kind of asexual "angelic" state to a lower material mode of living in the hierarchy of the created order, one theologian had a different view. Augustine of Hippo came to believe that, even without the Fall, Adam and Eve would have consummated their marriage and brought forth children. The result of the Fall for Augustine was not that men and women became sexual beings, but that "the uncontrollable elements in sexual desire revealed the working in the human person of a *concupiscentia carnis,* of a permanent flaw in the soul that tilted it irrevocably towards *the flesh....*With Adam's Fall, the soul lost the ability to summon up all of itself, in an undivided act of will, to love and praise God in all created things."[4] For Augustine, sexuality was a part of creation and not the mark of an imprisoned soul. At the same time, however, sexuality was forever flawed by the sin of Adam. Sexuality, therefore, "spoke, with terrible precision, of one single, decisive event within the soul. It echoed in the body the unalterable consequence of mankind's first sin."[5] It is this view of sexuality that we in the Western Church have inherited and which still informs our thinking today.

However, today we note with commendation the many Christians, both ordained and lay, who have taken vows of celibacy in order to better serve their callings as Christians. Many such persons serve with dignity and honor in our religious orders.

The Teaching of the Book of Common Prayer

The Augustinian understanding of sexuality was institutionalized in the Church. The celibate, monastic vocation was considered a higher calling than marriage. Marriage, though, was still a good as it served the ends of procreation and companionship while providing the remedy of sin. This is to say, marriage provided a context in which sexual desire, concupiscence, was properly restrained and served the human goods of the procreation of children and the companionship between husband and wife. This understanding of sexuality and marriage was first fully expressed in the Fourth Lateran Council of the Roman Catholic Church in 1214. It was, in turn, adopted in Anglicanism in the 1549 Prayer Book.

The Declaration of Intention

This understanding has since been modified. Title I, Canon 18, of the Episcopal Church requires that the priest shall ascertain that those to be married understand "...that Holy Matrimony is a physical and spiritual union of a man and a woman, entered into within the community of faith, by mutual consent of heart, mind, and will, and with intent that it be lifelong." Before being married, the woman and man are required to sign the following declaration:

We, A.B. and C.D., desiring to receive the blessing of Holy Matrimony in the Church, do solemnly declare that we hold marriage to be a lifelong union of husband and wife as it is set forth in the Book of Common Prayer.

We believe that the union of husband and wife, in heart, body, and mind, is intended by God for their mutual joy; for the help and comfort given one another in prosperity and adversity; and, when it is God's will, for the procreation of children and their nurture in the knowledge and love of the Lord.

And we do engage ourselves, so far as in us lies, to make our utmost effort to establish this relationship and to seek God's help thereto.

As we have seen, this tradition of sexuality and marriage is biblically based. It is especially grounded in the teaching of Jesus that marriage is a lifelong union. This Church has chosen to deal pastorally with those who divorce, but to be married, the intention must be lifelong union.

The canon declares that the purposes of marriage are companionship for mutual help, comfort, and joy; and for procreation and nurture of children, when God wills that the couple have children. This is the order of Genesis 2, endorsed by Jesus. It is a reversal of those Jewish traditions which considered the marriage a failure if there were no sons, and of those Christian traditions that have tended to consider sexual joy to be sinful, and procreation to be the only legitimate purpose of sex.

The Exhortation at a Marriage

The tradition of the Episcopal Church on human sexuality and marriage is embodied in the Exhortation read by the celebrant at the beginning of the liturgy. Marriage is the union of a man and a woman in a covenanted relationship established by God in creation. Although the equality of the woman and man is assumed, the "giving away" of the bride is still present as an option which may be used. (The first option, moreover, is a "presentation" in which both the bride and the groom may be presented for marriage.) Paul's teaching that the relationship between Christ and the Church is like that between bride and groom is cited to the honor of the marriage union.

Beginning the marriage service by reading the Exhortation to the congregation makes a definitive statement as to our understanding and teaching regarding marriage. The Exhortation is based upon Scripture of the Old and New Testaments and it is rooted in our tradition. Massey Shepherd, in his commentary on the 1928 Book of Common Prayer services, says:

> The Exhortation is a solemn and emphatic pronouncement of the sacredness of marriage, both as a divine institution given to humanity at its creation (Genesis 2:18, 24; *cf.* Matthew 19:5) and as a society redeemed and hallowed by Christ to be a type of that perfect love He has for His Church (Ephesians 5:22-23).

As Marion Hatchett points out in his commentary on the 1979 Book of Common Prayer, the 1549 Book of Common Prayer's Exhortation lists three reasons for the institution of marriage: (1) for the procreation of children; (2) as a remedy against sin (to avoid fornication); and (3) for mutual society, help, and comfort. The American Prayer Books did not include these purposes of marriage until the revision of 1979, and it was not until 1949 that the purpose of marriage was stated in a Declaration of Intention. Although our present Prayer Book omits "to avoid fornication" as one of the purposes of marriage, it does include as God's purposes for marriage mutual joy, help, and comfort given to one another, and the procreation of children.

The 1549 and successive English and American Prayer Books state that marriage is honored or honorable. This elevates marriage to the same status as was held by celibacy in the sixteenth century. It should be noted that the milieu of the early Church assumed an imminent eschatological end. In this context, and along with a negative view of sexual intercourse, celibacy was honored as an especially virtuous state, and marriage was somewhat of a concession for those who were burning with passion (1 Cor. 7:9). Clearly, the Book of Common Prayer holds up the covenant of marriage as a gift of God, intended to be entered into advisedly, reverently, deliberately, and in accordance with God's purposes.

Anglican thought no longer considers the procreation of children to be the sole purpose of sexual intercourse. As long ago as 1958, the Lambeth Conference stated:

> [T]he procreation of children is not the only purpose of marriage. Husbands and wives owe to each other and to the depth and stability of their families the duty to express, in sexual intercourse, the love which they bear and mean to bear to each other. Sexual intercourse is not by any means the only language of earthly love, but it is, in its full and right use, the most intimate and the most revealing; it has the depth of communication signified by the Biblical word so often used for it, "knowledge"; it is a giving and receiving in the unity of two free spirits which is in itself good (within the marriage bond) and mediates good to those who share it. Therefore it is utterly wrong to urge that, unless children are specifically desired, sexual intercourse is of the nature of sin. It is also wrong to say that such intercourse ought not to be engaged in except with the willing intention to procreate children.[6]

In fact, the one petition that may be omitted from the prayers in the marriage liturgy is, "Bestow on them, if it is your will, the gift and heritage of children..." (BCP, p. 429). Apparently, the couple, even if not past child-bearing years, have some choice in the matter. The ready access to contraception in the twentieth century has made this choice a reality, and the Church in its official teachings has urged its members to make that choice responsibly. This is especially imperative in light of the growing crisis of overpopulation, particularly in the Third World, as it relates to the well-being of the family.

The words "one flesh" are not used in the Exhortation, but the idea is clearly stated: "The union of husband and wife in heart, body, and mind is intended by God for their mutual joy, for the help and comfort given one another…and, when it is God's will, for the procreation of children and their nurture in the knowledge and love of the Lord." Christian marriage is clearly a covenanted relationship that includes not only the woman and man, but also God and the Church. This is not a private contract as might be drawn up by the individualistic secular culture in which we live. God has determined the nature of this institution, not we. Therefore the Church continues, in a changing secular world, to develop norms for life-long marital chastity and abstinence for the unmarried.

---

[1] Elaine Pagels, *Adam, Eve and the Serpent* (New York: Random House, 1988), p. 16.

[2] This teaching is reflected in the attitudes of present-day members of the Church. More than 95% (over 14,000 persons) of those participating in the human sexuality discussion questionnaire agreed or strongly agreed with the statement, "Human Sexuality is a gift from God and it is good."

[3] J. G. Davies, *The Early Christian Church*, pp. 244–245.

[4] Peter Brown, *The Body and Society* (New York: Columbia University Press, 1988), p. 418.

[5] *Ibid.*, p. 3.

[6] *The Family Today* (1958), p. 13.

5
THE DISCONTINUITIES

The 70th General Convention in Resolution A104sa, while affirming the Church's traditional teaching, speaks of "the **discontinuity** between this teaching [the traditional teaching of the Church] and the experience of many members of this body."

Christian marriage, as we have seen in the previous chapter, is a solemn and public covenant between a man and a woman in the presence of God and the only context the Church has recognized as appropriate for sexual intercourse. As witnesses to this covenant and by promising to uphold the two persons in the marriage, the parish community makes its own covenant with them, locating both the ceremony and the marriage itself in the context of Christian community and ongoing support (in intent if not always in reality). But what of the large number of persons and couples whose experience and relational status put them outside this covenant and in the state of discontinuity referred to in Resolution A104sa? Should the Church's agenda be set entirely by Scripture and tradition? Some say "yes"; others think informed reason and experience also have a role to play.

In this chapter we will look at the experience of those who have received God's gift of sexuality but are outside the covenant of marriage and we will also examine some of the findings of those social and biological scientists and psychologists whose work has challenged the traditional stance of the Church with regard to human sexuality.

Adolescent Sexuality

Adolescence is a time of intense interest in sexuality and of emerging sexual feelings, a time of curiosity and excitement, of apprehension and fear. At this time of sexual exploration and activity, which is natural and expected, the Church teaches that abstinence before marriage is virtuous. Intercourse, however, among teenagers is a problem. If adults refuse to acknowledge the occurrence of this sexual behavior, they cannot teach healthy, responsible behavior and decision making. Disconnected from these realities, we leave our teenagers to deal with their sexuality, a central aspect of their lives, with too little guidance from the Church. How might we better help and teach our children?

In contrast to the experience of previous generations, a large number of American teenagers are now sexually active. Figures released early in 1992 by the Division of Adolescent and School Health of the Centers for Disease Control show that 54% of high school students have had sexual intercourse. Boys are more likely than girls to have had sex, 61% to 48%.[1] Other federal findings indicate that the incidence of teenage pregnancy continues to rise. In 1989, 36.5 of every 1,000 girls ages 15 to 17 had a baby—up 8% from the previous year.[2]

Such figures are not surprising when we consider the ways in which young people are socialized to sexual activity in our society. Young boys are pressured to "score" and young girls are pressured to comply. For boys, sexual activity signals manhood. For girls, the defining event of womanhood is menstruation. Girls do not need sexual intercourse to convince them that they are women. While capable of powerful sexual arousal, they tend to be less interested in intercourse than in closeness and tenderness—in being loved. Girls have the most to lose as a result of pregnancy, but they are socialized to accommodate themselves to male wishes and desires. They have also traditionally been taught that they should preserve their virginity for their husband, and so they find themselves caught in the discontinuity of our society's mixed messages. Masturbation is also a phenomenon of sexual activity, one which has sometimes been seen as taboo or been associated with childhood sexual explorations, adolescence, and immaturity. Generally today in society, masturbation is recognized as part of both adolescent and adult sexuality. Unless it becomes compulsive, masturbation is not seen as physically and mentally harmful, but as a normal aspect of sexuality.

According to a new study of 34,706 Minnesota students in grades 7 through 12, more than one in four boys and girls enter adolescence unsure of their sexual identity, and by age 18, all but a few consider themselves either heterosexual or homosexual. Our society, however, acculturates all youth to presume they are heterosexual. Advertising, movies, romance novels, and virtually all of our educational programs (secular and religious) presume heterosexuality. For most of those adolescents who are homosexual, the already difficult adolescent experience becomes a nightmare.[3]

Unless gay/lesbian teenagers are fortunate enough to be associated with an unusually sensitive family, or school, Church, or community-center staff, they are likely to be surrounded by evasion and silence and to be consumed by inner and outer terror. Peer pressure leaves little space for anything but conformity, and most of the gays and lesbians who successfully negotiate their high-school years become expert at disguising their sexuality. For those who do not hide their identity, school days are filled with dirty looks, catcalls, half-whispered epithets, and cruel jokes, if not outright violence.[4]

Unfortunately, too many do not successfully negotiate these traumatic years. A study of youth suicide released in 1989 by the U.S. Department of Health and Human Services found that "gay youth are 2 or 3 times more likely to attempt suicide than other young people. They may comprise up to 30% of completed youth suicides."[5] Too many gay and lesbian youth face physical and verbal abuse and rejection from both peers and family. Having internalized societal negativity about homosexuality and not yet having sufficiently strong ego development and maturity to withstand the onslaught of abuse, gay youth are especially vulnerable to simply giving up on life. When everything you hear says that you are sick, bad, and wrong for being who you are, you can come to believe it.

Some religious groups are prominent among those who depict homosexuality as evil and sinful. Such religious beliefs may cause parents to force gay and lesbian youth to leave home and/or feel wicked, condemned to hell, and generally without hope. At present, many religious leaders are the least likely persons to be turned to for help in this situation and may be the least able to be truly helpful even if they are asked for assistance by youth and/or parents.

Both adolescent sexual identity and activity are pastoral matters to be addressed with compassion and informed concern. Through frank discussions, unhealthy behavior can be made conscious, and thus subject to responsible decision-making. In this way we help adolescents find the tools to make appropriate decisions. Church leaders, lay and ordained, willing to foster and facilitate such talk and learning within and among families and in youth and young-adult groups can begin the process by providing a safe environment in which young people can explore their sexual identities. Our challenge is pastoral: to help all youth, whatever their sexual identity and behavior, navigate the difficult journey from adolescence to adulthood.

Pre- and Postmarital Sexuality, Cohabitation, and Extramarital Sex

While the age at which teenagers become sexually active is declining, the average age for marriage is rising.

- Among women in general, the median age for first marriage in 1991 was 24.1—up from 20.8 in 1970.

- Among men, the median age was 26.3 in 1991 compared with 23.2 in 1970.[6]

Moreover, the number of people who are not married is increasing. In 1989 there were approximately 40 million single persons over the age of 18 in the United States, up from 21.4 million in 1970.[7] *The Janus Report on Sexual Behavior* (1993) reports that even among their respondents who classified themselves as "very religious," 70% acknowledged that they had premarital sexual experience. Among women who have never married, a 1992 survey indicated that 23.7% are mothers, up from 15.1% in 1982, with a particularly steep increase among educated and professional women (from 3.1% in 1982 to 8.3% in 1992).[8]

Census figures indicate that, as of 1989, there were 2,764,000 unmarried and unrelated opposite-sex couple households in the United States, as compared with 523,000 in 1970. Of these households, 858,000 contained children under 15 years of age (up from 196,000 in 1970).[9] Most of these cohabiting couples had never married but some, of course, included divorced and widowed individuals. (Data from the human sexuality dialogues in our own Church indicate that 87% of those responding know persons of both sexes living together without marriage. More than 70% of respondents said it was possible to be a faithful Christian and live with someone of the opposite sex without marriage.) Within the post-marital population of the U.S. in 1989, there were 14.6 million divorced persons (up from 4.3 million in 1970) and 13.8 million widowed persons (up from 11.8 million in 1970).[10] These statistics seem to indicate that many in our society—divorced, widowed, old, young, inexperienced—enter into relationships seeking to achieve intimacy without sacrificing independence.

Surveys indicate that many older persons today continue to experience sexual intimacy, continue to find it an important part of their lives. While frequency of sexual activity tends to decline and arousal tends to need increased interpersonal stimulation, older persons questioned say that their ability to reach orgasm has diminished little with age. Research indicates that more study needs to be done with regard to sex and the elderly, but it is at least clear that older persons should not be criticized for continuing to have sexual needs and interests.[11]

According to the National Opinion Research Center's General Social Survey, 71% of Americans believed in the early 1970s that extramarital sex was "always wrong." In the late 1980s, the percentage had increased to 76%. It is also the case that adultery appears in the criminal codes of many of the states, although these statutes are seldom, if ever, enforced.[12]

Apparently there is at least some discrepancy between belief and behavior, because affairs are not uncommon. A 1983 study found that 11% of husbands and 9% of wives reported at least one instance of extramarital sex in the previous year.[13] And a 1990 survey indicated that 31% of married Americans had had or were currently having an affair. On average these lasted almost a year. Only 17% of the men and 10% of the women then in an affair intended to leave their spouses. Even fewer (9% of men and 6% of women) planned to marry their current lovers. Two thirds of the men and 57% of the women said they didn't love their current lovers; "just a sexual fling," was said more often by men than women. Two thirds of the men and 40% of the women reported having had more than one affair. The surveyors also concluded that, "Adultery in contemporary America is as likely to occur in Manhattan, Kansas, as it is in Manhattan, New York."[14] Nevertheless, the Church and most of the population see it as still reasonable to expect fidelity within relationships once they are covenanted. Expectations about monogamous behavior, however, are best discussed openly rather than being assumed silently. Honestly admitting that all sexual behavior does not take place within marriage can open up the possibility of discussions about expectations during premarital counseling sessions as well as during the course of marriage.

A generation ago, most Episcopalians probably believed the Church's teaching confining sexual activity to marriage was being faithfully followed by the majority of its members. Some still believe this to be the case, but many know that it is not so. (Too many sons and daughters are or have been involved in live-in relationships without the benefit of marriage.) In some parts of the country, the vast majority of people marrying in the Church have been living together long before the service or are accustomed to sexual intimacy even if they don't live together. It is increasingly common, in fact, to see references to premarital sex being included within the protective cover of a "stretched" covenant of marriage—it's all right, as long as there is an "intent" to marry. Of course, many unmarried persons, whether living together or alone, have no such intention.

The popularity of social arrangements does not make them acceptable, but given the large number of single and cohabiting persons (whether by choice or circumstance), the need to postpone marriage for education and economic reasons, and birth control that works when properly used, many think it exceedingly optimistic of the Church to expect its young adults to refrain from sexual activity. Many also see it as unrealistic to expect all older single persons, divorced persons, and widowed persons to refrain from sex. (Those who participated in our human sexuality dialogues were about evenly divided on the question whether single persons should abstain from genital sexual relations, with about half saying yes and half saying no.) And given the current fragility of marital relationships and high

61

divorce rates, some argue that it is undesirable for the Church to pressure people into hasty marriages and remarriages in order for them to feel comfortable about being involved in responsible, intimate sexual relationships. Others continue to follow the teaching that under no circumstances may Church people be sexually active except within Holy Matrimony.

Adult Bisexuality and Homosexuality

The word "homosexuality" was first used in English in 1892; before that the terms used were "sexual inversion" or "sexual deviance." And not until the late 1940s, with the publication of Alfred Kinsey's 7-point scale, was there any general recognition among Americans of the complexity of sexuality. Based on his observations of sexual behavior and experience, Kinsey saw sexuality as a continuum rather than an either/or experience. He conceptualized a numerical scale ranging from exclusively heterosexual (to which he assigned the number 0) to exclusively homosexual (to which he assigned the number 6). In between came: (1) predominantly heterosexual, but incidentally homosexual; (2) predominantly heterosexual, but more than incidentally homosexual; (3) equally heterosexual and homosexual; (4) predominantly homosexual, but more than incidentally heterosexual; and (5) predominantly homosexual and incidentally heterosexual.

As Kinsey's scale approaches the half-century mark, it is useful for its simplicity, but specialists have begun to see it as an oversimplification. Over the years a number of other variables and elements for measuring sexual orientation have supplemented Kinsey's original model. Important among these findings is the observation that sexual orientation may be dynamic, not static, and that people, through inner-directed processes, may change with respect to their sexual orientation over time.[15]

Sexuality is experienced differently by everyone and "may be as changeable and unpredictable as other human appetites."[16]

Along with asexuality, bisexuality encompasses the middle range of Kinsey's scale. There are probably relatively few people who fall exactly in the middle, being equally attracted to men and women, falling in love equally with men and women, and having an equal number of male and female partners. In truth, bisexuality covers a wide range of experience/attraction from almost exclusive heterosexuality or homosexuality to occasional behavior, and persons in prisons who act homosexually only because heterosexual partners are unavailable. The issue is complicated by the fact that many people who engage in sexual activity with both men and women think of themselves as either heterosexual or homosexual, rather than bisexual. And a bisexual may recognize the possibility of being sexually intimate with either males or females but choose to act upon only sexual impulses with either same-sex or opposite-sex partners—or neither. It seems likely that persons who are bisexual more easily than others will be able to change their sexual behaviors by acts of choice and will.

True bisexuals often feel discriminated against and misunderstood by both homosexuals and heterosexuals. Being truly in the middle is a painful place. One interpreter has said that bisexuals do not so much escape the gay/straight split as "manage it"—or attempt to manage it—without having a consistent social experience upon which to build a consistent social identity.[17] However, as bisexuals grow older they tend to focus more and more exclusively on one sex or the other.[18]

Recent studies indicate a high level of bisexuality among women. One estimator has said that "on the basis of same- and opposite-sex behavior in adulthood, approximately 15% of women are bisexual and less than 1% exclusively homosexual."[19] It is possible, however, that pressure to marry may account for much of the heterosexual and bisexual behavior in the young adult lives of many lesbians. It is also possible that some of the dynamic nature of sexual orientation reported by some researchers and the element of change over time is, in fact, an aspect of the fluidity in the middle range of the Kinsey scale. Current research simply cannot provide certainty about these matters.

Homosexuality is one expression of sexuality, and the homosexually oriented person is one who is consistently attracted affectionally, romantically, and erotically to persons of the same sex. Persistent patterns of homosexual attraction, enduring experience of intimacy, and continuing manifestations of devoted love are the most trustworthy signs of sexual orientation, not simply genital activity.[20]

Contrary to popular belief, simply having homosexual fantasies, participating in oral and anal sex and/or having a homosexual encounter do not in and of themselves strongly suggest that one is homosexual. Heterosexuals may have both hetero- and homosexual fantasies and homosexuals may have both as well. Oral and anal sex are often associated with homosexuality, but, in fact, both are widespread practices among heterosexuals. It is also the case that the incidence of homosexual encounters on the part of heterosexuals is quite high.[21]

For both the heterosexual and homosexual person, the sexual aspect of one's being is only one portion of a complex identity and personality structure. Being primarily defined by their sexual orientation and behavior is distressing to most gays and lesbians, just as it would be for heterosexuals.

Determining the prevalence of homosexuality in the general population is very difficult, in part because of the complexity of determining who should be counted as homosexual. Should it be only those rating 4-6 on the Kinsey scale? Or should 2's and 3's be included? Furthermore, because of societal attitudes, vast numbers of gays and lesbians hide their identities from even

64

those closest to them. (Contrary to popular stereotypes, homosexual persons are not easily distinguishable from heterosexuals.) How then does one determine the true prevalence of homosexuality?

In spite of the difficulties, various estimating efforts have been made. For many years it was estimated, based on early Kinsey research, that up to 10% of the population may be homosexual. Given a population of 250 million in the United States, this means that upwards of 25 million people would fall into this category. Dr. Paul Gebhart, who continued Kinsey's work, suggested in the 1970s that a more likely estimate of the number of exclusively and predominantly homosexual persons would be in the range of 4% of adult males and 1–2% of adult women. Two surveys released in 1993 produced disparate results: *The Janus Report on Sexual Behavior* estimated that 9% of men and 5% of women are homosexual, while the Alan Guttmacher Institute estimated 1% for exclusively homosexual men.[22] Existing surveys do not provide information about the extent of homosexuality among ethnic groups in the United States. Also, in Central and South America, studies of actual sexual behavior, as distinct from officially recognized behavior, simply have not been made.

Casual homosexual contact and experimentation are not necessarily an indication of latent homosexual orientation, although these experiences often precipitate such fear. The estimates of incidental homosexual contact (one quarter to one third of all males having had one same-sex experience leading to orgasm since puberty) suggest one of the problematic areas of dealing frankly and honestly with the subject of homosexuality in our culture. It stands to reason that such anxieties will influence, if not compromise, reactions to suggestions that homosexuality be legitimized by the Church and by society. Of course, anxieties and fears faced and worked through with the help of priests, spiritual directors, and counselors can, in and of themselves, foster growth in self-understanding and be a channel of God's grace.

Homosexuality is found in all races, nationalities, ethnic groups and social classes, and in all periods of history from archaic civilizations to the present. But however universal and ancient the existence of homosexuality, it is also clear that the way in which sexual behaviors and orientations are lived out will not be the same in all cultures and moments in history. Sexual practices will not be the same, and the social forces that encourage or discourage them will not be the same. Anthropologists have shown us that many cultures around the world accept some form of homosexuality (transgenerational, transgenderal, or equalitarian), but the acceptance of one form does not imply the acceptance of other forms.[23]

Attitudes about homosexuality have varied greatly at different places at different times. (Among those who participated in the human sexuality dialogues in our own Church, 80% agreed or strongly agreed that homosexuality is a genuine orientation for some people and 66% said that gay men and lesbian women can be faithful Christians.) Oppression and tolerance have waxed and waned over the centuries as a consequence of social and economic developments, class anxieties and pressures, gender stereotypes, and notions of unequal power relations, domination, and exploitation. Ancient Greece, for example, countenanced homosexual relationships between married men who functioned as mentors and postpubescent youths. Important to this relationship was the disparity in age and the fact that the youth was always the passive partner. In the late Middle Ages, however, homosexuality was increasingly suppressed, a trend which has been linked to two distinct but related sources: a "growing preoccupation with homosexuality" as "an indirect and unanticipated consequence of the efforts of Church reformers to establish sacerdotal celibacy" and a middle-class morality that "became increasingly forceful in its opposition to a life-style of luxury and excess as class divisions widened."[24] In the first instance, clerical celibacy and the all-male communities it produced made homosexual activity more attractive and available. In the second instance, homosexuality had become identified with the wealthy and cultured classes. Historically, homosexuality has been deviant largely to the degree that society, at any given moment in time, has defined it as such—in other words, the status of homosexuality is historically and culturally conditioned.

Are homosexual persons born that way or are they the product of their environment or some combination of these factors? This vexing question, which is integral to our dialogue, remains unanswered at this writing, in spite of active research efforts in several fields, proliferating theories, and much interest from professionals and lay observers of all sexual orientations. In the physical sciences, researchers have explored hormonal links, differences in brain structure, and the possibility of a genetic component. The latter possibility has increased with the recent announcement that researchers have located the chromosomal area where they believe they will eventually isolate one or several genes that may predispose some men toward homosexuality. A recent study of the sexual orientation of twins suggests lesbianism also has a genetic basis.[25] Social scientists have offered explanations that include environmental factors and the role of social learning. Dr. John Money of Johns Hopkins University and others emphasize the interaction between biological and psycho-social factors. "Heterosexuality, homosexuality, and bisexuality," says Money, "all have both prenatal and later causes, which interact during critical periods of development to create a long-lasting or even immutable sexuoerotic status." Money also points out that it is incorrect to view prenatal influence as biological and postnatal as nonbiological. "Influences that reach the brain through the senses during social communication and learning are just as much biological as those that reach the brain through hormones circulating in the bloodstream of a fetus." William Byne and Bruce Parsons propose another interactional model "in which genes or hormones do not specify sexual orientation per se, but instead bias particular personality traits and thereby influence the manner in which an individual and his or her environment interact as sexual orientation and other personality characteristics unfold developmentally."[26] Some contend that the experience of incest, sexual abuse, and rape are important determinants of homosexuality. To date there is insufficient evidence to prove or disprove the extent of this influence. It does seem clear that the experience of abuse affects the choices of some bisexuals and persons in the mid-range of the Kinsey scale.

The political stakes and anxiety levels are high with regard to this issue of "cause" both in the Church and in society. Polls show that Americans who say individuals cannot change their homosexuality are much more affirming and supportive of gays and lesbians. On the other hand, many would like some one thing, social force, or group to blame. Mothers and fathers are always handy scapegoats and all too frequently impose that unhelpful burden on themselves. Many gays and lesbians report wanting desperately to understand "Why me?" at some stage of their coming to terms with the reality of their sexual orientation. Later in their journey, they frequently cease to care very much about how they got that way and focus instead on leading a happy, well-adjusted life and, for Christians, a life focused on relationships with God, partner, family, and the community at large. Often, members of the Church community in seeking "the cause" are really wanting "a cure." Might the Church's energy, instead, be focused on the persons who need to be loved, nurtured, cherished, accepted, and supported, including gays, lesbians and their families?

Regardless of one's sexual orientation, the development of sexual identity, while intense in adolescence, is a lifelong process. Even if one is "certain" of one's identity in early adulthood, it is not uncommon to make unexpected discoveries about oneself later in life. Gay men and lesbians often, even as young children, have a feeling of being different from their same-sex peers. They often feel like "outsiders" in relation to peers and even to family. Progress in self-discovery for some people is slowed or thwarted entirely by patterns of denial fostered and exacerbated by Church and societal negativity. Women may identify their same-sex feelings as "special friendships" and men as "normal" male bonding. "Feeling in love" is a common beginning point for the struggle with homosexual-identity issues. But, even if there are no such feelings, no actual change in sexual identity, the process of integration of identity for everyone goes on throughout adulthood. Often the process moves from a period of identity confusion through stages of increasing awareness, toleration, acceptance, and pride to a synthesis in which sexual orientation is seen as important but as only one aspect of the self. Self-disclosure becomes almost automatic as a greater security is felt in the identity, and interaction in the heterosexual world is experienced as generally rewarding.

In the best of situations, Christians will see this process as one aspect of their lifelong spiritual journey. Clergy and Church friends can play an important role in creating a safe environment and supporting gay/lesbian parishioners through this critical life passage. Sometimes the Church as institution and Church people are more hindrance than help. Making an effort to understand the process of identity formation is one step toward learning how to care pastorally for gays and lesbians.

An Examination of Some Assumptions Concerning Homosexuality

Assumption #1: Homosexuality is a choice.

While there is not yet agreement on its **cause,** recent research does not suggest that homosexuality is a **choice.** Dr. John Money puts it this way: "Despite popular assumptions, homosexuality, heterosexuality, and bisexuality are not preferences. Each is a sexuoerotic orientation or status. They are no more chosen than a native language is."[27] "Choice" may enter the picture for bisexuals, who often attempt to choose either a heterosexual or a homosexual way of life.

It is very difficult, especially considering the particular way in which women have been socialized to accommodate themselves to family and societal expectations, to determine what really is "choice" and what is social conditioning. But women's sexual orientation seems to have a fluidity that leads some researchers to speculate that bisexuality may be more common among women than men and therefore more "choice" is available to women than to most men. At this point, there is no knowing if this is true.

It is frequently the case that homosexual persons feel social pressure (both internalized and externalized) to repress or deny their sexual feelings. This can be very harmful because repression tends to intensify feelings; it can also cause depression, disassociation, and other problems. Social and religious pressures are especially problematic if homosexuals are counseled or pressured into marriages that may eventually fail or continue amid much emotional pain, leaving human wreckage along the way.

Assumption #2: Gays and lesbians are marginal members of society, both in numbers and contributions.

Any subset of American population that accounts for anywhere from 2.5 to 25 million people cannot be considered insignificant. (There are approximately 2.4 million Episcopalians in the United States.) Even though homosexual persons remain invisible for the most part, gays and lesbians are, in fact, everywhere. They may be your own child, your doctor, your lawyer, your psychologist, your carpenter, your electrician, your colleague at work. They are among the business people, teachers, social workers, nurses, and hospice volunteers of our communities. And they are in our churches—in the pew and in the pulpit. The business community is increasingly interested in homosexual couples as an important market—"double income, no kids"—although estimates of the number of children being raised by homosexual parents, the majority of whom are "invisible," range from 6 million to 14 million.

Assumption #3: Gays and lesbians are psychologically "sick."

In 1973, the American Psychiatric Association removed homosexuality from the Diagnostic and Statistical Manual of Psychiatric Disorders, its official list of mental illnesses. The American Psychological Association adopted a similar resolution in 1975. In addition, researchers have failed to discern any demonstrable psychopathology in their homosexual samples, nor have they been able to differentiate homosexual from heterosexual subjects, suggesting that there is no greater pathology or tendency toward psychological maladjustment among homosexuals than heterosexuals. Other studies have found that adolescent gays, as we have already indicated, may be very vulnerable to suicide.[28] Finally, new studies show that children raised in gay and lesbian households are no more likely to have psychological problems than those raised in more conventional circumstances.[29] Even so, some Freudian-based theory still considers homosexuality immature, although Freud himself made it clear that homosexuals must not be treated as "sick" simply because of their homosexuality.[30]

Assumption #4: Gays and lesbians are child molesters.

Numerically, far more child molesters are heterosexual than homosexual. Recent studies indicate that only 6.8% of those who molest male children are homosexual, while 38.6% are exclusively heterosexual, and 54.4% are bisexual. For those who molest female children the number who are homosexual is 2.6%, while 63.6% are exclusively heterosexual and 33.8% bisexual.[31] Reliable studies indicate that most child molesters are married and that most victims are female children, although some men victimize both boys and girls. Pedophilia is a serious psychological disorder whose victims repeatedly molest prepubescent children because they are sexually attracted to children. Molesters, who are most frequently male, are sometimes attracted to adults as well as children but most often to children alone. Among other sexual exploiters are ephebophiles—those adults sexually attracted to postpubescent teenagers.

Assumption #5: Gays and lesbians are sexually hyperactive.

An investigation of sexual activity in lesbian, gay, heterosexual-cohabiting, and married couples published in 1983 found that for the first several years of a relationship gay men had sex with their primary partner more often than heterosexuals did, but later on male couples showed a reverse pattern of lower sexual frequency than heterosexuals. In all four groups frequency declines with the duration of the relationship, leading the investigators to conclude that both physical aging and habituation independently acted to reduce sexual frequency.[32] There is evidence that "average sexual frequency is lower among lesbian couples than among gay male couples, heterosexual cohabitors, or married heterosexuals." Researchers trace this to traditional socialization that represses women's sexual expression (in lesbian couples both partners have been so socialized) and the fact that women place more emphasis on such non-genital sexual activities as hugging and cuddling.[33]

It is also the case that single lesbians have less frequent sex and fewer different partners than gay men, at least prior to the AIDS crisis which has changed sexual patterns for gay men. Lesbians have about the same rates of non-monogamy in long-term relationships as do heterosexuals—28% report at least one extrarelational episode. Before the AIDS crisis, gay males had the highest rates of extrarelational sex and often did so by mutual agreement, minimizing the breakup of relationships.[34]

It should also be noted that society contributes to patterns of homosexual behavior by driving it underground due to fear of discovery and the social sanctions that would result.

Assumption #6: Gays are feminized men and lesbians masculine women.

Scientists reject as too simplistic the equation that masculinity in a man and femininity in a woman equals heterosexuality and that the reverse equals homosexuality. It is sometimes the case that gender uneasiness or dissatisfaction occurs with a homosexual orientation but by no means always. A 1979 study of college students, for example, found no relationship between sexual orientation and masculinity or femininity.[35] There does seem to be a connection between early gender nonconformity (such as a boy preferring to play with dolls instead of engaging in rough, aggressive games) and the development of sexual orientation, but it is not a necessary determinant.[36]

Stereotypes would have us believe that within homosexual relationships "butch-femme" roles, modeled on a heterosexual frame of reference, are widespread. There is some evidence that this was the case in an earlier era, at least for women. But current research suggests that lesbians and gays actively reject rigid conformity to traditional husband-wife roles. Instead, there tends to be a sharing of responsibilities, household tasks, and decision making. Specialization occurs, but it develops individually, according to skills and interests.[37]

Assumption #7: Gays and lesbians can be "reoriented" to heterosexuality.

Freud grew to believe that it was as difficult to convert a "fully developed homosexual into a heterosexual" as to do the reverse."[38] Indeed there is no convincing evidence that homosexuals who are 5 and 6 on the Kinsey scale can be truly reoriented. Some are convinced, however, that with sufficient religious motivation, genuine shifts can and do take place. Some Christians involved in ministries such as Exodus and Regeneration have experienced such shifts in behavior and have given clear testimony to Church bodies on the subject. In the early 1970s psychiatrist Jerome Frank estimated that somewhere between 10 and 20% of exclusively-homosexual persons "can be helped to shift significantly." He also estimated that for bisexuals, up to 40% could become "essentially heterosexual." The absolutely essential element, he said, to any shift is a "high degree of motivation and cooperativeness." That the motivation is so crucial suggests that under no circumstances should anyone be coerced into treatment.[39]

Clinical studies indicate, however, that such treatment may result in serious problems such as severe anxiety and depression due to the disruption of a lifelong process of sexual identity formation and from injury to the patient's self-esteem. Richard Isay of the Cornell Medical College and the Columbia Center for Psychoanalytic Training and Research recommends analysis carried out with "appropriate neutrality" and "positive regard" for the client as a way to "ease the burden that society has imposed" and help the homosexual person resolve conflicts.[40]

Assumption #8: Gay men hate women and lesbians hate men.

The vast majority of gay men have exceptionally good relationships with women gay and heterosexual, and lesbians with both heterosexual and gay men. One of the outstanding characteristics of these relationships is the absence of sexual suggestion or innuendo. Often they are refreshingly ordinary relationships; sometimes deep friendships are involved and sometimes very comfortable brother/sister-like sharing becomes possible.

The relationships between gay men and heterosexual men are sometimes strained by sexual anxiety and psychological conflict. As mentioned above, the incidence of casual homosexual encounter is high for all men, especially among youth, and this fact makes uneasiness all the more a potential among adult males. The fact is that these relationships are probably no more sexualized than male/female relationships. And, fortunately, it is often not a factor at all, and fine, nonsexual friendships—personal and professional—are not uncommon for gay and heterosexual men. Lesbians and heterosexual women often seem to feel less anxiety relationally, probably because women are so highly motivated to make connections and to be related.

Homosexual Relationships

Since 1976, persons of homosexual orientation have been considered by the General Convention of the Episcopal Church to be "children of God who have a full and equal claim with all other persons upon the love, acceptance, and pastoral concern and care of the Church." At the same time, many in the Church are deeply troubled about open homosexual relationships, which are the visible expression of homosexuality. Single gays and lesbians, for the most part, blend into the primary heterosexual culture and go about their sexually active or inactive lives in an unobserved manner, just as do the millions of single heterosexuals. Gays and lesbians who are openly coupled bear the burden of their visibility, acting as lightning rods and attracting the "electricity" of censure. This has put the Church in the position of advocating committed, long-term, monogamous relationships (i.e., marriage) and, in fact, seeing them as the only legitimate context for sexual expression—but exclusively for heterosexuals.

All people have a need for acceptance, approval, affiliation, and deep connection. Close relationships have been heralded in verse, song, literature of all kinds—including Holy Scripture—throughout human history. They are heralded as well by health professionals as being important to health and well-being. Dr. Blair Justice, a psychologist at the University of Texas School of Public Health in Houston, observes, "It may be more important to have at least one person with whom we can share open and honest thoughts and feelings than it is to have a whole network of more superficial relationships."[41] As with all persons, homosexuals need and struggle toward a life of integrity, wholeness, companionship, and community—with little support from a culture caught up in the secular spirit of our times. For all baptized persons, the Church is called to be that support.

Like their heterosexual counterparts, most lesbian women and gay men want to have enduring, close relationships—the majority consider it of great importance to have "a permanent living arrangement" with a partner.[42] Researchers have also found that "most gay men and lesbians perceive their close relationships as satisfying and that levels of love and satisfaction are similar for homosexual and heterosexual couples who are matched on age and other relevant characteristics." A study of only monogamous couples found that "gay, lesbian, and heterosexual married partners were indistinguishable from one another" on love for partner and relationship satisfaction scores.[43] Clearly the desire for, and living-out of, "strength in need, a counselor in perplexity, a comfort in sorrow, and a companion in joy" is far more broad than many imagine.

As is the case with heterosexuals, there are homosexuals who are in exploitive and/or abusive relationships, and there are, as well, gay and lesbian couples in growth-fostering relationships. In growth-fostering relationships, both partners feel a greater sense of vitality and energy. Each feels more able to act and does act, each has a more accurate picture of her/himself and the other, each feels a greater sense of worth, each feels more connected to the other and has a greater motivation for connections with other people beyond the primary relationship.[44]

For homosexuals, as for heterosexuals, the desire to be in a relationship is not simply a desire for self-gratification and self-pleasure. Rather, it is about "journeying toward and joining in something that thereby becomes greater than the separate selves."[45] Relationship is about love, commitment, sharing activities and spirituality, closeness, touching, hugging, laughing, thoughtfulness, generosity, trustworthiness—and sometimes sexual intimacy. Our society's focus on sex in relationships, especially in gay and lesbian relationships, is out of proportion with reality and should not be used as a definitional criterion. This is not to say that sexual intimacy is unimportant in primary, committed relationships. In homosexual as in heterosexual relationships, intimacy is an important aspect of the bonding and nonverbal communication that allows relationships to transcend the ordinariness of daily life and to touch the eternal. In so doing, sexual intimacy strengthens committed love relationships.

In heterosexual relationships, women and men agree to love and care for each other. And no one disputes that such relationships have a spiritual dimension. The same kind of love, caring, commitment and spirituality characterize homosexual relationships as well, as has been heard in hours of Church testimony before Church commissions and conventions. In long-term, committed relationships—in which love is freely given and freely accepted—gays and lesbians can and do experience the identification of their love with Jesus Christ and of their relationships with his life. As it can be for heterosexual persons, the experience of steadfast love can be for homosexual persons an experience of God.

Homosexuals in Traditional Marriages

It is not at all uncommon for homosexual persons to be involved in traditional marriages. The pressures of peer socialization, family and religious constraints, and just plain unconsciousness in individuals, all conspire to lead both men and women to do what is expected of them at a certain age. Some men and women, unable to accept their homosexuality, intentionally marry hoping that will "cure" them; others find traditional marriage a convenient disguise for continued homosexual encounter. Some homosexuals marry and restrict their sexual contacts to their spouses but while having intercourse imagine the spouse to be a same-sex partner. Sometimes men, and especially women, are unaware of their same-sex attractions until later in life, after many years in a traditional marriage. Their testimony bears witness to the power of denial and rationalization. Others may recognize same-sex attractions as episodic or transitional and not necessarily definitive of the marriage.

When the homosexual orientation of one partner becomes apparent, typical reactions are to hide it, attempt to change it, or to pretend it does not exist. Relationships that take this route very frequently come apart over time, though sometimes couples are able to remain together while living relatively separate lives. Marriages in which both partners initially are unconsciously gay/lesbian are not at all uncommon. It seems possible, in fact, that such persons unconsciously are drawn to one another. Sometimes these relationships end in separation and/or divorce when awareness dawns, but sometimes, especially when parental responsibilities are a factor, a way to cope and stay together evolves. This is most possible when a strong friendship forms the basis of the relationship.

From time to time it is possible for mixed couples, most frequently heterosexual women and gay men, to learn to meet both partners' sexual and emotional needs and thus become able to live together very consciously and contentedly. Sometimes this accommodation is worked out only after alternating periods of separations and reconciliation. Compatibility, mutual interests and acceptance, the desire to raise children together, and a shared need for companionship contribute to the success of such relationships. It seems evident, however, that a high degree of psychological maturity is required of both partners.[46]

Skillful pastors and counselors can help couples do sexual identity work before, during, and after marriage. Homosexuality is often an unrecognized issue in pastoral counseling with the separated and divorced and their children.

Fear and Violence

The fear and intolerance of and violence against gays and lesbians that is growing at an alarming rate is a way of denying that homosexuals are of the same human kind as everyone else. It is also a well-known psychological defense mechanism that assures the perpetrator that he or she is not homosexual and does not share the feelings being observed in gays and lesbians. As one commentator has put it: "As long as we are inculcated with the terror of our own secret desires, we will try to beat them out of others when we cannot kill them in ourselves."[47] Researchers have shown that the greater the resemblance of the supposed homosexual or homosexuals to the in-group or the attacker, the greater the likelihood of hate-filled reaction.[48] In addition, new findings by psychologists suggest that the greatest portion of anti-homosexual bias "arises from a combination of fear and self-righteousness in which homosexuals are perceived as contemptible threats to a moral universe." The largest group among people who are biased, says Dr. Gregory Herek, a psychologist at the University of California at Davis, are those for whom homosexuals "stand as a proxy for all that is evil. Such people see hating gay men and lesbians as a litmus test for being a moral person." Such attitudes are supported, researchers say, by institutionalized bias which makes it officially permissible to hate gays and lesbians. All too often, attitudes in the Church contribute to this institutionalized bias and allow people to see homosexuals "as legitimate targets which can be openly attacked."[49] Observes Virginia Seminary ethicist David Scott, "While one can believe and teach that homosexual practice contradicts God's will without being homophobic, nevertheless much opposition and violence against gays and lesbians is motivated by irrational fears and hatreds."[50]

---

[1] Robert Byrd, "Most Students Aren't Virgins, CDC Reports," Associated Press, January 4, 1992. The survey included 11,631 high school students.

[2] Robert Pear, "Bigger Number of New Mothers Are Unmarried," *New York Times,* December 4, 1991.

[3] Report of article from *Burlington Free Press,* April 7, 1992, in *Pediatrics,* April 1992.

[4] Mary B. W. Tabor, "For Gay High-School Seniors, Nightmare Is Almost Over," *New York Times,* June 14, 1992.

[5] Paul Gibson, "Gay Male and Lesbian Youth Suicide," *Report of the Secretary's Task Force on Youth Suicide,* Vol. III (Washington, DC: 1989), pp. 110-142.

[6] Sara E. Rix, Ed., *The American Woman, 1990-91: A Status Report* (New York, 1990), Table 6, p. 369; U.S. Bureau of the Census, *Statistical Abstract of the United States: 1991* (Washington, DC: 1991), Table 50, p. 43.

[7] *Ibid.*

[8] *New York Times,* July 14, 1993.

[9] *Statistical Abstract of the United States: 1991,* Table 53, p. 44.

[10] *Ibid.,* Table 50, p. 43.

[11] Samuel S. Janus and Cynthia L. Janus, *The Janus Report on Sexual Behavior* (New York, 1993), pp. 23–27.

[12] Andrew Greeley, "Sex and Society: Time for a Reappraisal," *Boston Sunday Globe,* September 15, 1991; William E. Schmidt, "Adultery as a Crime," *New York Times,* April 30, 1990.

[13] Philip Blumstein and Pepper Schwartz, "Intimate Relationships and the Creation of Sexuality," in David P. McWhirter, Stephanie A. Sanders, and June M. Reinisch, eds., *Homosexuality/Heterosexuality: Concepts of Sexual Orientation* (New York: Oxford University Press, 1990), p. 317.

[14] James Patterson and Peter Kim, *The Day America Told the Truth* (New York: 1991), pp. 94-99.

[15] Fritz Klein, "The Need to View Sexual Orientation as a Multivariable Process: A Theoretical Perspective," in McWhirter et al., eds., *op. cit.,* pp. 278-81. See also essays by Whalen, Geary, and Johnson; Pillard; Coleman; and Nichols in the same collection.

[16] Rebecca Nahas and Myra Turley, *The New Couple* (New York: 1979), p. 8.

[17] Mariana Valaverde, *Sex, Power, and Pleasure* (Toronto: University of Toronto Press, 1985), pp. 115-116.

[18] Wayne R. Dynes, ed., *Encyclopedia of Homosexuality* (New York: 1990).

[19] Margaret Nichols, "Lesbian Relationships: Implications for the Study of Sexuality and Gender," in McWhirter et al., eds., *op. cit.,* pp. 354-356.

[20] James Zullo and James Whitehead, "The Christian Body and Homosexual Maturity," in Robert Nugent, ed., *A Challenge to Love* (New York: 1983), p. 26.

[21] In 1979, Masters and Johnson reported that the third most frequent fantasy of male homosexuals is of heterosexual contact; the fourth most frequent fantasy of heterosexual males and the fifth most frequent fantasy of heterosexual females is of homosexual activity. William H. Master and Virginia E. Johnson, *Homosexuality in Perspective* (Boston: 1979), p. 178. In 1990, when James Patterson and Peter Kim asked 2,000 at 50 locations across the country about their fantasies, 75% of the men and 14% of the women had fantasies of having anal sex (40% of the men and 34% of the women reporting these fantasies said they had lived out the fantasy). Patterson and Kim, pp. 77, 81. See also June M. Reinisch and Bruce Beasley, *The Kinsey Institute New Report on Sex* (New York: 1990), pp. 132-33, 136, 139-140.

[22] Paul H. Gebhart, "Incidence of Overt Homosexuality in the United States and Western Europe," in National Institute of Mental Health Task Force on Homosexuality, *Final Report and Background Papers* (Washington, DC: 1972), pp. 22-29.

[23] See David F. Greenberg, *The Construction of Homosexuality* (Chicago: University of Chicago Press, 1988).

[24] Greenberg, *op. cit.,* p. 280.

[25] New York Times, July 16, 1993; *Archives of General Psychiatry,* 50 (March 1993):217–223. See also, "Is Homosexuality Biologically Influenced?" *Scientific American,* Vol. 270, No. 5 (May 1994): 43-55.

[26] John Money, "The Development of Sexual Orientation," *Harvard Medical School Health Letter* (June 1992), p. 7; William Byne and Bruce Parsons, "Human Sexual Orientation: The Biologic Theories Reappraised, *Archives of General Psychiatry,* 50 (March 1993), 236–237.

[27] *Ibid.,* p. 4; on the subject of "choice," see also Richard A. Posner, *Sex and Reason* (New York: Cambridge University Press, 1992), pp. 296-300.

[28] See Evelyn Hooker, "The Adjustment of the Male Overt Homosexual," *Journal of Projective Techniques,* Vol. 21, pp. 18-31; P. F. Reiss, "Psychological Tests in Homosexuality," in Judd Marmor, ed., *Homosexual Behavior* (New York: 1980), pp. 296-311; and Lawrence A. Kurdek and J. Patrick Schmitt, "Relationship Quality of Partners in Heterosexual Married, Heterosexual Cohabiting, and Gay/Lesbian Relationships," *Journal of Personality and Social Psychology,* Vol. 51 (1986), pp. 715-717.

[29] *New York Times,* December 2, 1992.

[30] Richard Isay, "Psychoanalytic Theory and the Therapy of Gay Men," in McWhirter et al., eds., *op. cit.,* pp. 283-284.

[31] Dr. Gene G. Abel, Behavior Medicine Institute of Atlanta, in a report presented to the American Psychiatric Association, May 1993.

[32] Blumstein and Schwartz, pp. 315; 319, note 5; 316.

[33] Letitia Anne Peplan and Susan D. Cochran, "A Relationship Perspective in Homosexuality," in McWhirter et al., *op. cit.,* p. 337; Blumstein and Schwartz, p. 316.

[34] Margaret Nichols, p. 357.

[35] Bancroft, p. 104; Louis Gooren, "Biomedical Theories of Sexual Orientation: A Critical Examination," in McWhirter et al., *op. cit.,* p. 72; Michael D. Storms, "Sex Role Identity and Its Relationships to Sex Role Attributes and Sex Role Stereotypes," *Journal of Personality and Social Psychology,* Vol. 37 (1979), pp. 1779-1789.

[36] Bancroft, p. 104; for an extended treatment of gender nonconformity and homosexuality, see Alan P. Bell, Martin S. Weinberg, and Sue Kiefer Hammersmith, *Sexual Preference* (Bloomington: Indiana University Press, 1981).

[37] Peplan and Cochran, p. 344. See also the series of tables related to this subject in Bell and Weinberg, Appendix C, pp. 323-325.

[38] Sigmund Freud, *Standard Edition of the Complete Psychological Works* (London: 1953-1974), Vol. 18, p. 151.

[39] Jerome D. Frank, "Treatment of Homosexuals," in National Institute of Mental Health Task Force on Homosexuality, *op. cit.,* pp. 64, 66-67.

[40] Isay, pp. 285-86, 287, 300.

[41] As quoted in the *New York Times,* February 5, 1992. In a study of heart patients published in early 1992 in the *Journal of the American Medical Association,* researchers from Duke University Medical Center found that those who lacked a spouse or confidante were three times as likely to die within five years of diagnosis as were the patients who were married or had a close friend.

[42] Bell and Weinberg, p. 322. In surveys (by Bell and Weinberg and three others), between 40 and 60% of the gay men questioned were currently involved in a steady relationship; in the current AIDS era, the figures are even higher. In most studies, the proportion of lesbians in an ongoing relationship was close to 75%.

[43] Peplan and Cochran, p. 332-33; Kurdek and Schmitt, p. 717.

[44] These characteristics of growth-fostering relationships were developed by Jean Baker Miller. See her "What Do We Mean by Relationship?" *Stone Center Work in Progress # 29* (Wellesley: 1986), p. 3.

[45] Judith V. Jordan, "Clarity in Connection: Emphatic Knowing, Desire, and Sexuality," *Stone Center Work in Progress #29* (Wellesley: 1987), p. 11.

[46] See Rebecca Nachas and Myra Tulley, *The New Couple: Women and Gay Men* (New York: 1979).

[47] Darrell Yates Rist, "Sex on the Brain: Are Homosexuals Born That Way?" The *Nation,* October 19, 1992, p. 429.

[48] Dr. Keith Brodie, Address of the President of Duke University to the Freshman Class, August, 1989. A study of heterosexual male college students found that students who had negative views of homosexuality were more aggressive toward homosexual targets they believed to be similar to themselves than toward those they considered dissimilar. When the targets were heterosexual, the response pattern was just the opposite: subjects were far more aggressive to those they believed to be dissimilar to themselves than to those they believed similar. See Christopher L. San Miguel and James Millham, "The Role of Cognitive and Situational Variables in Aggression toward Homosexuals," *Journal of Homosexuality,* Vol. 2 (1976), pp. 11-27; and Greenberg, pp. 447-448.

[49] Daniel Goleman, "Homophobia: Scientists Find Clues to Its Roots," *New York Times,* July 10, 1990.

[50] Letter to the Rt. Rev. Harry W. Shipps, March 4, 1994.

6
SEXUALIZED VIOLENCE:
The Use and Abuse of Power

Even as we affirm and celebrate the positive, life-enhancing nature of our human sexuality, our discussion is incomplete unless we acknowledge that what God intends for good, we can use for ill. What is meant to be life-affirming can, and does, becoming death-dealing. Violence against women, sexual exploitation, and sexual abuse are issues that demand attention and informed action. Our discussion here, while intentionally limited in scope, is a reminder that more is required. Our purpose in this chapter is to broaden the discourse on human sexuality by looking, however briefly, at how sex is used as a weapon of domination instead of a way of expressing love and mutuality.

A Different Reality

The traditional Christian teaching that human sexuality is a sacred gift from God, and that Christian marriage is created for companionship, mutual help, comfort, and joy, does not, unfortunately, match the experience of many women and their children who live and survive in another reality. Theirs is a reality in which God's gift of sexuality has been desecrated—transformed from a holy, sacred expression of love and connection into a weapon of intimidation and destruction.

Daily media accounts of incest, child sexual abuse, molestations, pedophilia, beatings, rapes, and murders underscore the reality that, for far too many women and children, the home is not a place of comfort, safety, and joy, but rather a dangerous, life-threatening environment. Home in the United States is a place where, according to a 1987 epidemiological study, "wife beating results in more injuries that require medical treatment than rape, auto accidents and muggings combined."[1] And home for children is no safer when 1 out of 4 girls and 1 out of 6 boys are sexually abused before they are 18, most likely by the age of 11.[2] Lest we think, if we are not victims, we are not affected, Dr. Judith Herman, a leading expert on sexual violence and recovery (writing almost a decade ago), states that, "Rates of sexual assault on women are sufficiently high that [many] women live with a pervasive fear of violence . . . [Such] fear," she concludes, "affects women's psychological development."[3] Even if they are not victims, some women can, and do, live lives constricted by this apprehension.

No longer safe, these homes have become a place of terror. Such terror is described in a report from the United States Senate Judiciary Committee hearings on proposed legislation, the Violence Against Women Act. This report states that over "1 million women were attacked by their husbands and lovers last year, and an additional estimated 3 million violent domestic crimes—murders, rapes, and assaults—went unreported."

Power, Not Sex

It is this fear-ridden world of sex and violence that we, as a community of faith, must confront. Rape, incest, child sexual abuse, and the exploitation of vulnerable adults or children by clergy and other professionals are not sexual acts, they are sexualized acts of violence perpetrated by those with power against those who are powerless and vulnerable. Unfortunately, most people today do not understand that rape is not a sexual act. Such an understanding could facilitate society's and the Church's work of reconciling the discontinuity between Christian teachings that affirm and celebrate human sexuality as good and the lived experience of millions of women, girls and boys.

Clergy Sexual Misconduct

The number of clergy sexual misconduct cases has increased dramatically in recent years within all denominations. The skeleton is out of the closet. According to the Church Insurance Company's report on the year 1992, "Sexual misconduct has real costs. In the past ten years, the Church Insurance Company has paid an aggregate of $7.9 million on sexual misconduct cases." While we can measure the cost in dollars it is more difficult to measure the cost in terms of human loss.

How we understand and face up to discussions of why and how this could happen will determine whether we make real and lasting progress toward eliminating the sexual exploitation of people who trust us. We have made enormous strides in how we respond to both the victim and the abuser, but more can and should be done. Frequently, survivors of incest will describe, with incredible sadness, feelings of having had their childhood stolen. Survivors of clergy sexual abuse, in similar fashion, describe feelings of having had their souls stolen. The betrayal of trust inherent in both incest and clergy sexual abuse is profoundly damaging to the survivor, the abuser, and the parish family, who sometimes knows the story but more often feels the pain without knowing why. The damage to all has serious and long-lasting implications, for the recovery of trust and the restoration of one's faith is not easy to achieve.

Sex as Commodity

In addition to sexualized violence, sex for money or sex as a commodity is also a perversion of God's gift to us of our sexuality. Prostitution, pornography, and some hard-sell advertising are several ways in which sex is for sale. Sex becomes a commodity—sex sells, we buy. And such sex is big business. In the United States, pornography alone is estimated to be a $20 billion a year industry, exploiting and dehumanizing women and children.[4]

Prostitution, the oldest and the most unchanged profession on earth, is as prevalent in Christian countries and societies as in non-Christian ones, and is demonstrably alive and well in 20th-century America. While the prostitute is reviled, we seldom deal with the fact that there are many more customers than there are prostitutes. The alarming connection between prostitution and childhood sexual abuse previously suspected is increasingly supported by research. A report from the National Network of Women's Funds Seventh Annual Conference on Violence Against Women (1991) stated:

> There are approximately 1 million adult prostitutes in the United States. Most were recruited or coerced into prostitution before they reached 18 years of age . . . Most have run away from home and been forced into prostitution in order to support themselves . . . Most have been victims of childhood sexual abuse, incest, rape, and/or battery prior to entering prostitution . . . In addition to the 1 million adult prostitutes, there are approximately 1.2 million children used in the sex industry in this country. Although estimates vary due to the covert nature of child sexual exploitation, without effective intervention most of these children will grow up to be adult prostitutes.[5]

To live into and out of a Christian understanding, we must both affirm and strive for a full expression of the God-given goodness of our human sexuality and confront and reject the ugly perversion of God's gift that sexualized violence is. Our willingness to live within the tension both actions engender—to stand with those whose lives are shattered—will help us seek out, name, and discard the historical and cultural patterns we have inherited that condone and perpetuate the systems that abuse. Such abuse is not only individual pathology but also corporate dysfunction built around a closely held secret. Approaching our task with both courage and humility may unexpectedly reveal a moment in which we will see clearly how and when we, in the Church, can provide comfort, and when we don't, how we betray the trust given to us. Perhaps then we can choose—as God intends us to—to be a place of healing, a sanctuary, for all.

[1] E. Stark and Flitcraft, "Violence Among Intimates: An Epidemiological Review," 1987, quoted in *A Wind of Change: Funders Working to End Violence Against Women,* A Report of the National Network of Women's Funds Seventh Annual Conference, Chicago, April 18-21, 1991.

[2] *A Wind of Change: Funders Working to End Violence Against Women,* A Report from the National Network of Women's Funds Seventh Annual Conference, Chicago, April 18-21, 1991.

[3] Judith Lewis Herman, M.D., "Sexual Violence," Working Paper No. 8, the Stone Center, Wellesley College, Wellesley, MA, 1985.

[4] Michael Gershel, "Evaluating a Proposed Civil Rights Approach to Pornography: Legal Analysis as If Women Mattered," quoted in *A Wind of Change,* Fact Sheet.

[5] *A Wind of Change,* p. 18.

7
PASTORAL GUIDELINES

Statements from General Convention

We acknowledge that General Convention has made the following statements concerning issues of human sexuality and the conduct to which we are called:

A. "Homosexual persons are children of God who have a full and equal claim with all other persons upon the love, acceptance, and pastoral care of the Church." (General Convention, 1976)

B. "That this [1979] General Convention recommend to Bishops, Pastors, Vestries, Commissions on Ministry and Standing Committees, the following considerations as they continue to exercise their proper canonical functions in the selection and approval of persons for ordination:

1. There are many conditions, some of them in the area of sexuality, which bear upon a person's suitability for ordination;

2. Every ordinand is expected to lead a life which is 'a wholesome example to all people.' (Book of Common Prayer, pp. 517, 532, 544) There should be no barrier to the ordination of qualified persons of either heterosexual or homosexual orientation whose behavior the Church considers wholesome;

3.   We reaffirm the traditional teaching of the Church on marriage, marital fidelity, and sexual chastity as the standards of Christian sexual morality. Candidates for ordination are expected to conform to this standard. Therefore, we believe it is not appropriate for this Church to ordain a practicing homosexual, or any person who is engaged in heterosexual relations outside of marriage."

C. "Physical, sexual expression is appropriate only within the lifelong, monogamous union of husband and wife in heart, body, and mind intended by God for their mutual joy; for the help and comfort given one another in prosperity and adversity and, when it is God's will, for the procreation of children and their nurture in the knowledge and love of the Lord as set forth in the Book of Common Prayer, and . . . that this Church continue to work to reconcile the discontinuity between this teaching and experience of many members of this body . . ." (General Convention, 1991)

Guidelines While We Continue the Dialogue

Community life in our Anglican Communion includes the need to respect both the unity and the diversity of our communion. Respect means that the Episcopal Church will maintain recognizable, faithful Anglican norms in our teaching regarding sexuality. Diversity means understanding with pastoral sensitivity the different experiences of people within our own Church and within other Churches of the Communion. During the continuation of the dialogue and discussion in the Episcopal Church on human sexuality and the Christian response, we are particularly called to live and act in a manner which is both open to the leading of the Spirit and grounded in our historic faith. To that end, and mindful of our collegiality in the House of Bishops, we commend the following guiding principles for our actions as a Church during this period.

1. We recognize that, while our sexuality is a very important part of who we are, it is not all of who we are, or even the most important part of who we are. In fact, it is not necessary to be sexually active to be fully human. It is also the case that moral behavior bears upon the question of sanctity and whether our sexual behavior is or is not consistent with the gospel life.

2. We recognize that while there are a variety of approaches to sexual ethics in the Bible, the standard found in the New Testament of lifelong, monogamous, heterosexual union as the setting intended by God for sexual relationships between men and women is the foundation on which the Church's traditional teaching is built.

3. We acknowledge that standards or norms have existed for our sexual conduct, and that these standards or norms—as approved, modified, and amended—are understood as faithful guides for Christians in matters related to sexuality. These standards and norms exist to enable us to act in accordance with the ethical and moral implications of the Christian faith and to shape us, given our natures and circumstances, into the fullness of the stature of Christ.

4. We continue in study and dialogue, seeking to reconcile, to the extent possible, discontinuities which

may exist in the area of human sexuality between Scripture, tradition, and informed reason on the one hand, and our human experience on the other.

5. We are convinced through our study of human sexuality that a significant minority of persons are homosexual. Therefore it is necessary for the Church to articulate appropriate moral and ethical guidelines for homosexual as well as heterosexual Christians.

6. We believe sexual relationships reach their fullest potential for good and minimize their capacity for ill when in the context of chaste, faithful, and committed lifelong unions between husband and wife. There are those who believe this is as true for homosexual as for heterosexual relationships and that such relationships need and should receive the pastoral care of the Church.

7. We view as contrary to the baptismal covenant, and therefore morally unacceptable, sexual behavior which is adulterous, promiscuous, abusive, or exploitative in nature, or which involves children or others incapable of informed, mutual consent and understanding the consequences of such a relationship.

8. We acknowledge that certain discontinuities exist, in human sexuality as well as in other areas, between the standards and norms set forth by the Church's teaching and the experience of a number of the Church's members. Those discontinuities, of necessity do not interrupt the communion we share. Where we disagree, we need to continue the dialogue. Therefore we commit ourselves to:

a. Respond pastorally to those persons whose sexual behavior does not conform to the traditional standards and norms of the Church.

b. Continue in trust and *koinonia* ordaining only persons we believe to be a wholesome example to their people, according to the standards and norms set forth by the Church's teaching.

c. Hold paramount the belief that we are all loved equally by God and are called to love one another.

d. Commit to ongoing consultation concerning these matters with the wider Anglican Communion and with our ecumenical partners.

APPENDIX

A REPORT ON THE HUMAN SEXUALITY DIALOGUES

This Appendix to the Pastoral Study Document was prepared by the National Steering Committee for the human sexuality dialogues at the request of the Pastoral Teaching Committee.

Resolved, That this General Convention commissions the Bishops and members of each Diocesan Deputation to initiate a means for all congregations in their jurisdiction to enter into dialogue and deepen their understanding of these complex issues [regarding human sexuality]; and further this General Convention directs the President of each Province to appoint one Bishop, one lay deputy and one clerical deputy in that province to facilitate the process, to receive reports from the dioceses at each meeting of their provincial synod and report to the 71st General Convention. (The Fourth Resolve of the 1991 General Convention Resolution A104sa.)

Background

The 1991 General Convention in the Fourth Resolve of Resolution A104sa assigned to "the Bishops and members of each Diocesan Deputation" the task of developing the means and encouraging "all congregations in their jurisdiction to enter into dialogue" on the complex issues surrounding human sexuality.

97

Furthermore, the Convention took the unusual action of assigning directly to the Provinces the task of facilitating the process, receiving reports from the several dioceses, and reporting back to the 1994 General Convention.

At their meeting in the fall of 1991, the Presidents and Vice-Presidents of the Provinces responded to the Fourth Resolve by agreeing to establish in each Province a Steering Committee made up of a Bishop, one clerical Deputy and one lay Deputy who would oversee the project in their Province. (At least one Province, Province VII, had already begun its work.) Further, the Presidents and Vice-Presidents established a national Steering Committee to be made up of persons serving on the Steering Committees of Provinces II, VII, and VIII. The Rt. Rev. O'Kelley Whitaker, then President of Province II, was asked to chair the National Steering Committee, often called "the Whitaker Committee" to distinguish it from the group dealing with the Fifth Resolve—on the Pastoral Teaching—chaired by the Rt. Rev. Richard F. Grein, Bishop of New York. The latter committee has popularly become known as "the Grein Committee." Throughout the process, the chairs of the two committees have maintained full communication on the work of the respective groups.

The first task of the National Steering Committee on Resolution A104sa was to develop a clear understanding of its task and to interpret as best it could for itself and for the Church the intent of General Convention in the Resolution. To that end, a Context Statement was developed and distributed to all Bishops and Convention Deputies in a mailing dated March 23, 1992. This was the first of eight mailings from the national Steering Committee distributed periodically throughout the study time. However, because of limited funds available, subsequent mailings were sent only to diocesan Bishops and to Provincial Steering Committees.

The Context Statement sought to be very clear about our task and responsibilities:

1. We were not being asked to conduct a popular referendum on current attitudes on human sexuality in the Church.

2. We were called to enable and encourage dialogue, including discussions among people who may hold different perspectives.

3. We understood dialogue to be different from debate, the latter being an occasion for trying to convince others of one's own position, and the former being a time for conversation that involves honest listening as well as charitable speaking.

4. While recognizing that issues relating to gay and lesbian persons are of great concern both in the Church and in society in general, we saw our task as much broader, upholding all concerns about sex and gender.

We saw it incumbent upon us (a) to develop or identify existing materials to be made available to the several dioceses to be used at their discretion; (b) to make possible training opportunities for diocesan leaders who, in turn, would offer training to leaders in congregations; and (c) to develop a means by which the learnings from this process could be gathered. We recognized we were being asked to work in a highly charged area. To move from the prevailing "debate mode" into the "conversational" mode would not be easy. Everyone would need the opportunity to explore new skills, new ways of dealing with one another on sometimes volatile issues.

Many possible studies on human sexuality were reviewed by the members of the Whitaker Committee. Some were found to be focused upon one or a few areas of human sexuality. A few, in our opinion, seemed too narrow in their treatment of the issues.

The study, "Human Sexuality and the Christian Faith," prepared by the Evangelical Lutheran Church in America, working in much the same climate as we were, met our criteria in nearly all respects. Augsburg Fortress, the Publishing House of the ELCA, was enormously helpful in permitting us to use this study freely, to replace a chapter with one designed for Episcopal participants, and even to print the Episcopal Edition at much less cost than we could have it done elsewhere. We experienced a warm ecumenical spirit of cooperation in sharing this study.

At the same time, Province VII, which had moved ahead in responding to Resolution A104sa, had already engaged a consultant team to prepare a special study in response to the Resolution. The national Steering Committee had the opportunity to join in the process of the development of "Human Sexuality: A Christian Perspective." The cost of the production of this study was borne by Province VII.

Thus, we had two excellent, yet different, studies to offer the Church. *At the same time, we made it clear that any diocese that chose to utilize other material should feel free to do so.* The same reporting instrument would provide the opportunity for input no matter what study material was used.

Recognizing that Spanish is the second language most often used in the Episcopal Church, we proceeded to develop Spanish language translations of the two studies as well as of the reporting instruments. Here again, Augsburg Fortress readily made available to us the Spanish language translation of their material, a great saving to us.

The National Steering Committee has operated as an instrument of the Provinces in their response to General Convention. At the same time, since General Convention provided no funding for this project and Provinces usually do not have such resources, we appealed to the Presiding Bishop to seek funding for a budget of approximately $30,000, which he was graciously able to do. Major expenditures included mailings, support of leadership training, consultancy, and Spanish translations.

Data Gathering Process

In preparing an instrument to gather data from parishes and dioceses, the Committee agreed on these principles:

1. The questions should be general in nature so that they could be responded to by parish participants regardless of the discussion materials the group had used.

2. The questions, the Committee agreed, were not referendums on Church policy, theology, or legislation. Rather the questions were to gather the opinions of those who participated in the discussion program reflecting ways in which the participants' ideas had been reinforced or changed as a consequence of the discussions. A place for write-in comments and observations was to be included in the questionnaire format as well.

3. Limited funding and the press of time required that the means of tabulating and collating the individual responses should be rapid and completed with a minimum expenditure of funds or effort on the part of parishes, dioceses, or provinces.

The Questionnaire

The earliest drafts of the questionnaire were prepared by Warren Ramshaw, a lay member of the Whitaker committee. The whole Committee revised question wording, question order, and suggested new questions not previously included. Committee members were asked to try out the questions on parish groups to see if the question wording was clear and unambiguous. The questions were examined and commented upon by parishioners in Southern Virginia, in Central New York, in Rochester, in several places in Province VII and in Province VIII. Additionally, comments and revisions were suggested by participants in the leadership training programs in three different parts of the country. Individuals and groups with special interests in the topics addressed in the questionnaire made further suggestions for improving the questions. Finally, the Committee examined revised drafts of the instrument, paying particular attention to its form, clarity and ease of use.

To facilitate the collection of data it was decided to take advantage of the pyramidal structure of the Church as a route of successive levels of reporting. Parishes were provided with a questionnaire tally sheet on which they could indicate the number of persons answering each question and the way the question was answered. Parishes were then instructed to send the individual questionnaire forms and the summary sheet to their diocesan offices where a new set of tallies were made summarizing the responses from all the parishes in the diocese. These forms were sent on, then, to a designated person in each province, reporting the answers given for all the participating parishes in the diocese. The dioceses were asked to keep the individual questionnaires to await later instructions on their disposition.

Next, the provinces, using a form especially prepared for them, summarized the numbers of individuals who answered each question in a given way for the reporting dioceses in that province. Finally, the persons in each province responsible for the compilation of the diocesan data forwarded a single report with their totals to the Whitaker Committee.

This method of summarizing totals on successive levels has the advantage of being relatively rapid and accomplished with little cost in time or funds to the participants on any of the three levels. The disadvantage of that method, however, is that cross-cutting analysis of the data is not possible. Another method of answering these kinds of questions has been developed to provide for cross-cutting analysis. For the same reasons, the write-in responses to the three questions at the end of the questionnaire form cannot be summarized in this three-level method.

For that reason, the Committee asked each participating diocese to send its individual questionnaire response forms to a central point where they could be entered into a computer data base. It is fortuitous for the Committee that a small number of volunteers made themselves available to computerize all the data from each individual's questionnaire. This has been an extraordinary task. There were 86 variables for each of the 15,342 persons to be entered, an operation that began early in July and continued essentially on a daily basis to the middle of December in 1993. This data collection is independent of the one developed through the triangulation method described earlier. The computer based data has fewer individuals included in it than the triangulation method because we received fewer questionnaires from the dioceses than were tabulated by the triangulation method. Remarkably, the percentages in these two data sources are nearly identical on all items. Both sources provide clear and unambiguous data for our analysis. In this same process the write-in responses (Part B) have been read and a large sample of them have been recorded, omitting duplications.

What the Responses Tell Us

Characteristics of Respondents

Those responding to the human sexuality questionnaire do not necessarily constitute a representative sample of Episcopalians in all parts of the country. These responses are not intended to speak for the whole Church on any of these topics. Rather, these are the responses of those who have participated in the discussions on human sexuality in our parishes, a program generally consisting of five two-hour sessions. These persons have read the material their parishes elected to use and they have completed the questionnaire form. Moreover, the potential responding population is further screened by the fact that some dioceses chose to participate in this national program and some did not. Further, even in participating dioceses some parishes chose to undertake the discussion program and some did not. Finally, even in participating congregations only a small proportion of the entire parish membership actually participated.

The number of responses reported in studies from groups as large as those participating in this process are very rare indeed. A measure of the opinions of this number of Episcopalians on *any* topic has not been undertaken before. (For a comparison, the studies of the attitudes of the whole Church membership done by the Committee on the State of the Church and reported in the *Blue Book* for the 1982 and the 1985 General Conventions were based on a randomly drawn sample of 1,000 Episcopalians.)

Responses were received from 18,219 persons by the triangulation method and the following general descriptive statements are based on those responses. (While we have written responses indicating the participation of between fifteen and twenty thousand persons in the discussions groups, we estimate that by the sale of discussion guide materials, that nearly 30,000 persons were involved as leaders and participants in some way in this dialogue process.) As many as 1,128 parishes and slightly more than seventy-seven per cent of the dioceses participated in discussions and forwarded information through the provinces to the Committee. The Chaplains of the Armed Forces participated as well in seven groups in various parts of the world, adding sixty-three responses.

Demographically, half of the respondents are in the age category 40 to 59. Two per cent (358 persons) are over 80 and slightly more than one percent (208 persons) are under 20 years of age. Ninety-three per cent of the responses come from lay persons. Seven per cent are from ordained persons. Slightly more than half of the respondents are married. Eight per cent are divorced and thirteen per cent are divorced and remarried. Eleven per cent were never married.

Characteristics of the Discussion Groups

Sixty per cent of the discussion groups met for five sessions with another twenty-three per cent meeting six times. Half of the respondents used the study guide: "Human Sexuality and the Christian Faith," the ELCA publication. Thirty-five per cent used the guide: "Human Sexuality: A Christian Perspective," the curriculum prepared by Province VII. The remaining fifteen per cent used other material or combinations of these resources. Just under forty per cent of those responding reported attending five sessions of the discussion groups and nearly thirty per cent more attended four.

The topics most frequently included in the discussions were these: Biblical understanding of sexuality, Christian marriage and family, psychological and social aspects of sexuality, and gay and lesbian relationships. These topics were followed in rank order by discussions of gender—the social consequences of being male or female—and the Anglican/Episcopal views of sexuality.

The climate of the discussion groups is described by nearly sixty per cent of the respondents as always free and open. Another thirty per cent report their groups were usually but not always free and open. Only two per cent say their group experience was often or most always painful or difficult.

Forty-five per cent say the leadership of their group was very effective (5 on a scale of 5 to 1). Thirty-four per cent rate the leadership as a 4. Thus, nearly eighty per cent of the respondents find the leadership of their groups very good. More than eighty per cent agree or strongly agree that their discussion group is made up of a wide variety of persons with different life experience, people who are quite different from each other. Sixteen per cent disagree with that description of their group.

Learning and Outcomes

In naming the topics in which the participants believe that they have grown as a result of the study and discussion program in which they have participated, the most frequent response is Biblical understandings of human sexuality. This response is followed, in order, by the Church's teachings on human sexuality, and by understandings of gay and lesbian relationships.

To help participants focus on specific persons they know who can be thought of in sexual categories, they were asked if they know persons—friends or relatives—whom they understand to be in one or another of a listed set of categories. The Committee felt this question was useful to help respondents recall that lists of sexual categories are more than disembodied cells but rather are statements about persons, some of whom the respondents know.

In this question the most frequent responses indicate everyone knows persons who are married, divorced, or divorced and remarried. Next most frequently identified as persons they know are those who are single by choice, gay men, persons of opposite sex living together although not married, and persons sexually active outside of marriage.

Under what circumstances is it possible to be a faithful Christian and be identified in one or another sexual category? Almost one hundred per cent of the respondents say that one can be a faithful Christian and be divorced or divorced and remarried. Three quarters report that one can be faithful and live with someone of the opposite sex without marriage. Seventy per cent indicate that being sexually active as a gay or lesbian person is not contrary to being a faithful Christian. Respondents are equally divided in affirming or denying that bisexual persons can be faithful Christians.

Responses to other items on which the opinions of respondents were asked can be grouped by degrees of agreement or disagreement with a series of questionnaire statements. More than 85 per cent say they *strongly agree* or *agree* with these assertions:

- Human sexuality is a gift from God and it is good (96%)

- Sexual abuse is a major problem in the United States (90%)

- The Church should take an active and responsible role in teaching young people about human sexual issues (92%)

- Women and men should be equals in the Church (90%)

- Gender should not be a factor in determining people's daily work and vocation (87%)

Less widely affirmed, these statements are strongly agreed *or* agreed *to by 50 to 85 per cent of the respondents:*

- Homosexuality is a genuine sexual orientation for some people (81%)

- The chief standard for right and wrong is not specific texts but the character of Jesus revealed in the Gospels (80%)

- Single people should abstain from genital sexual relations (57%)

- Supporting committed relationships between gay or lesbian persons could strengthen the Christian community (53%)

- If I were single, I would abstain from genital sexual relations (50%)

At the same time, the respondents disagree with some of these assertions. Respondents disagree *or* strongly disagree *with the following statements:*

- The Bible teaches that men and women are not equal (87%)

- Short term sexual relationships are acceptable if both adult parties agree to participate in them (64%)

- It is more important for the Church to offer guidance on *what* to think about human sexual issues than on *how* to think about them (52%)

Further Analysis

Using the computer-based data (15,342 persons), a number of other relationships and insights can be gleaned. All of the relationships reported here are statistically significant. (That is, there is less than one chance in one thousand that the reported relationships are produced by chance. Rather, the statements are significant because there is a *real* relationship between the reported variables.)

- 64% of the lay persons in the study are women and 23% of the ordained persons are women;

- 75% of ordained persons and 59% of lay persons disagree that it is more important for the Church to offer guidance on *what* to think on human sexual issues than on *how* to think about them;

- Women are much more likely (62%) than men (43%) to agree that they would abstain from genital sexual relations if they were single;

- At every age level from 20 to 80, there is increasing agreement that the respondents would abstain from genital sexual relations if they were single;

- A greater proportion of women than men, and ordained persons than lay persons believe that homosexuality is a genuine sexual orientation for some people;

- Agreement with the belief that supporting committed relationships between gay or lesbian persons could strengthen the Christian community is greater among women than men, among ordained persons than lay persons, and among young persons than older persons;

- Men more than women and young persons more than older persons agree that short term sexual relationships are acceptable if both adult parties agree to participate in them.

Summary and Conclusions

The responses from thousands of Episcopalians who have participated in the study and discussion of issues in human sexuality understood within the context of a Christian perspective show a range of belief and opinion which exists within the Church today. Those who have completed the study questionnaire acknowledge that they have grown most in Biblical understandings of human sexuality, the Church's teachings on those issues, and in their understandings of gay and lesbian relationships. They affirm that human sexuality is a gift from God and it is good. While affirming that homosexuality is a genuine sexual orientation for some people, they also say that single people should abstain from genital sexual relations, which may be contradictory conclusions. A slight majority of the respondents say that supporting committed relationships between gay or lesbian persons could strengthen the Christian community. A substantial majority reject the idea that the Bible teaches that men and women are unequal or that short term sexual relationships are acceptable if they are agreed to by the participants.

For all of the respondents these issues of human sexual behavior are personalized by the large number of friends and/or relatives they acknowledged who fitted various sexual categories or descriptions. For such people the topic of human sexuality and Christian perspective is not an abstraction. It is part of their own awareness of these issues while attempting themselves to become faithful Christians.

The original Context Statement prepared by the Whitaker Committee as an explanation and guide to the discussion process and released in March, 1992, in part, says this:

> We are being called to a dialogue, including discussions with people who may hold different perspectives. A dialogue is not a debate, not an occasion for seeking to convince others of the rightness of our position and the wrongness of theirs. Rather, it is an opportunity to be open with each other, both to share our own insights and to listen carefully to those of others. It is time to discern the leading of God's Spirit.

The descriptions of their discussion groups by the respondents, the topics they discussed, and the areas in which they claim growth all appear to approach the goals of that statement.

One layman from Province VIII, age 20-39, has written this in commenting on his experience in dialogue: "The study itself was quite bold and yet at the same time refreshing to see. The Church has taken its first step in addressing some much needed issues."

DISCUSSION GUIDE

for

CONTINUING THE DIALOGUE

**A Pastoral Study Document of the
House of Bishops
to the Church as the Church Considers
Issues of Human Sexuality**

PREFACE

The following "Discussion Guide for Continuing the Dialogue" is a partial response to General Convention Resolution B 12a (Indianapolis, 1994). The General Convention mandated a national interim Committee for Dialogue on Human Sexuality "to enable continuing dialogue by providing a variety of resources as it may deem appropriate, by providing training for dialogue leaders, by maintaining contact with the several dioceses, and by keeping the dioceses and provinces informed of dialogue in process throughout the Church, reporting to the 72nd General Convention."

The resolution called on "Bishops and Deputies to this General Convention to work to establish within their respective jurisdictions the means to encourage and enable the widest possible study and conversation on *Continuing the Dialogue: A Pastoral Study Document of the House of Bishops to the Church as the Church Considers Issues of Human Sexuality.*"

In providing the Discussion Guide, the members of the Committee have attempted to identify issues and raise questions that will promote dialogue and theological reflection. Additional resources will be made available throughout the triennium.

In Christ,

The Rt. Rev. Craig B. Anderson   The Rev. Jane N. Garrett
Co-chair   Co-chair
        Committee for Dialogue on Human Sexuality

SUGGESTIONS FOR DISCUSSION

TO THE LEADERS:

The Summary of each chapter is best read aloud before the group considers the Questions.

Be aware that group members may have had personal and painful experiences relating to the topics being discussed. On the one hand, people should not be pressured to talk when they would rather remain silent. On the other hand, this group is not for therapy. Nor is it a TV talk show situation. Be prepared to offer participants a resource for counseling or therapy outside the group.

TO THE GROUP MEMBERS:

This is a conversation in which we listen and talk, not a debate in which we win or lose. While we expect to disagree with some of the opinions of others in the group, differing views are honored as valid for that person and should not be argued. We will show the same respect that we expect to receive.

We speak from our own experience, using "I..." statements, rather than generalizing about people ("They...") or speaking for others ("You...").

We all have the right to privacy. We can choose to speak or to keep silent at any point in the conversation. It is not OK to pressure others to talk, or to ask personal questions.

Let us respect confidentiality. Please do not repeat anything said or discussed in the group in such a way as would reveal who the speaker was—unless you have that person's explicit permission. *General* characterizations of what was discussed *are* permitted.

#1 THE DIALOGUE TODAY IN THE EPISCOPAL CHURCH

SUMMARY:

This denomination, like other Christian groups of our time, is spending much of its corporate energy on issues of human sexuality and behavior. Historic Church teachings about topics such as marriage have not been consistent with the life experience of many of our members. Attempts to use legislation have not fully resolved the discontinuities perceived by many between the Church teachings on questions of human intimacy and actual modern Christians' experiences. In each age we have had to experience the discomfort that comes when our assumptions about the nature of the world are challenged. We found, with Galileo, that the universe does not revolve around us. We found, with Darwin, that creation is more complicated than a literal reading of Genesis. We decided that divorce should not keep people from the sacraments. More recently, in the decision to allow women full participation in the Church, we decided that gender alone need not dictate all our opportunities.

Today the House of Bishops is commending a pastoral approach of asking us to live together in charitable tension, to enter into dialogue and attempt to deepen our understanding of these complex issues. As Christians we can speak with each other about the realities of our lives, with prayerful consideration of the implications of the Baptismal Covenant which we share.

QUESTIONS:

What changes have you experienced in your own congregations in your lifetime? How were they positive or negative?

How have these changes impacted your personal practice of your faith?

#2 DIALOGUE IN COMMUNITY

SUMMARY:

The basis of our communion—what we have in common—is our faith in Jesus Christ, our baptism, our shared worship, and our shared life. When we focus on what we have in common, we find it easier to remember that what unites us is far greater than the issues that divide us. It is a sign of maturity to be able to bring the richness of differing perspectives to bear on our discussions and to live with ambiguity while we seek clarity together.

Our best resource for working with complex issues in the Church is to have communities of committed Christians who are willing to discuss their concerns in an open dialogue. This discussion needs to happen in a setting that is safe, and that safety comes when we feel that our communion with each other is sustained by the Holy Spirit.

The Scriptures teach us that the Body of Christ, our Church, is made up of many different members, and that we are all interdependent and all equally important. When we are mindful of this, disagreement about issues which are not central to our Christian faith cannot disrupt our commitment to a loving community.

QUESTIONS:

What experience have you had in living or working with people who hold opinions strongly at odds with your own?

How would you describe what unites us as Christians? As Episcopalians?

Is it easier to describe those things that divide us than those things we have in common? Why or why not?

#3 THE BIBLE

SUMMARY:

The Scriptures are seen as the Word of God because God inspired their human authors, and because God still speaks to us through their words. The Scriptures were composed over a span of twelve centuries by people who reflected the societies of their time. The central theme of the Bible is the call to worship a God who demands justice and righteousness and who is full of compassion and mercy. Understanding these varied and sometimes contradictory writings calls for our use of reason and tradition. Reason here means bringing prayerful, rational reflection to the written word in the light of human experience and learning. Tradition is the record of our beliefs over time, and roots us in our history. While we can enrich our lives by personal study of the Bible, we also need the balance of exploring it with other Christians. This is how we can avoid imposing our own biases and assumptions on its meaning, or taking individual parts out of their context in the great themes of the Bible.

It is no surprise, given the historic nature of the Bible, to find teachings about sexual behavior that seem foreign to us today. Examples include the assumption that women and children are property, fears of ritual impurity from contact with sexual fluids, or the avoidance of acts associated with competing religions. Yet the Bible does have messages that speak clearly to us today:

- We are created as sexual people who can join together to become "one flesh" and can give one another joy, comfort and support.

- We can share with our Creator in the process of bringing new life into the world.

- Faithful living is all of a piece, and all human relations are meant to find their deepest value in the context of their response to God's love.

However our sexual behavior, like all our behaviors, has the potential for harm as well as for blessing.

QUESTIONS:

The Bible sees sexual behavior as a community concern, especially when it comes to anything relating to procreation or to the keeping of ritual purity. Our culture sees sexual behavior as a more private matter unless it involves abuse of other people. To what extent do you think the sexual behavior of Christians is a matter of concern for others in the Christian community?

What difference does Jesus' ministry make in how matters of sexuality are approached?

Are there parts of the Bible you personally find confusing? Why?

#4 MARRIAGE

SUMMARY:

The Episcopal Church states that Holy Matrimony is a physical and spiritual union of a man and a woman, entered into within the community of faith, by mutual consent of heart, mind and will, and with the intent that it be lifelong. This union is "intended by God for their mutual joy; for the help and comfort given one another in prosperity and adversity;" and, as a voluntary outcome, "the procreation of children and their nurture in the knowledge and love of the Lord" (BCP page 423). Our tradition has held that sexual intimacy is only appropriate within such a relationship.

We have built upon and modified Scripture and tradition about marriage. We have rejected the norms that women are property and that the production of sons is the primary goal of marriage. The emphasis on a lifelong commitment reflects Jesus' radical challenge to the rights of men to cast aside wives for any reason. We have rejected traditions that justified sexual passion only through the procreation of children, and have seen companionship as a primary purpose of marriage. We have grown away from the early Christian beliefs that the rejection of sexual passion was the highest good, and no longer see celibacy as a more honorable state of life than marriage. And we have moved from the view of marriage as a contract between families concerning property rights to a view of marriage as a covenant among a woman, a man, the Church, and God.

QUESTIONS:

How can the Church most effectively prepare persons for the sacrament of marriage?

How can the Church support its norm of marriage as a life-long commitment with the cultural realities of divorce?

The mobility of our society makes it unlikely that many newly married couples will remain in the community that witnessed their marriage. How can the Church fulfill its pledge to "support these two people in their life together" when they are no longer rooted in one place?

What difference do non-traditional relationships make to the sacredness of marriage? What difference do they make to the couple?

#5 DISCONTINUITIES

SUMMARY:

All of us need close relationships in which we give and receive acceptance, approval and deep connection. This presence of someone who is "strength in need, a counselor in perplexity, a comfort in sorrow, and a companion in joy" is necessary for our health and well-being. Those of us who are baptized need the Church to be the support for our relationships. We need help in countering the cultural obsession with sex that denies the wholeness of love, commitment and sharing that can accompany sexual intimacy. The official teaching of the Church confines sexual intimacy to marriage, yet many single persons of all ages have experienced sexual intimacy in a relationship not blessed by the Church. The Church thus finds itself torn between wanting to keep a clear rule about when sexual intimacy is permissible and recognizing that many of its members do not live by this rule.

The complexity of human sexuality has hardly been touched on in adolescent religious education. Sexual exploration becomes for many a way of confirming their identity as male or female, and for navigating the ten to fifteen years between sexual maturity and marriage. Our gay, lesbian, and bisexual children face even more danger as they look for acceptance in a culture that condemns them, and they are the group of teens most subject to the hopelessness and despair that leads to suicide. Often the Church is the last place they turn for help.

QUESTIONS:

Think back to your childhood religious environment. What did you learn about expectations for sexual behavior by men and women? What were the messages about appropriate roles for men and women? What do you find in your learning that was helpful or harmful? What, if anything, should we teach today about religion and sexuality?

Refer to the eight "Assumptions Concerning Homosexuality" in this chapter, pages 70-76. Reflect on the differing viewpoints, and on your own assumptions.

What messages about sex does our culture promote? How might the Church respond?

What can the Church do to lessen hatred and violence toward homosexual persons?

#6 SEXUALIZED VIOLENCE: THE USE AND ABUSE OF POWER

SUMMARY:

What God has given us for good we can use instead for ill. We can use sex as a weapon of domination instead of as a way of expressing love and mutuality. Violence against women and children, including sexual violence, is commonplace in our culture. The Church has been directly involved in the misuse of sex as some in authority have asserted the power invested in them by the Church and betrayed the trust inherent in their positions by exploiting people sexually. In addition, we have habitually blamed victims for the problems created by commercial sex and not the customers who make this exploitation of women and children profitable. We must seek out, name and discard the patterns in our culture and in our congregations that support this abuse of others.

QUESTIONS:

What factors can you find in our religious and cultural history that might be used in an attempt to justify sexual violence? How can we educate our members of all ages to prevent or overcome the attitudes that lead to abuse?

If someone who had been abused sought support from your congregation, what would the response be? What do you think it should be?

What are the implications when a member's trust in the Church is betrayed by someone in the institution who had been seen as a source of help and comfort? What is the impact on the person betrayed, the one doing the betrayal, and the total community?

What guidelines does your diocese have for preventing sexual misconduct by clergy and lay employees and church workers?

#7 PASTORAL GUIDELINES

During the continuation of the dialogue and discussion in the Episcopal Church on human sexuality and the Christian response, we are called to live and act in a manner which is both open to the leading of the Spirit and grounded in our historic faith. To that end eight guiding principles for our actions as a Church are commended by the House of Bishops.

Please read "Chapter 7—Pastoral Guidelines" (pages 91-95) in its entirety.

QUESTIONS:

About which (if any) of the "Guidelines While We Continue the Dialogue" are you particularly enthusiastic? To which do you take exception?

What is our responsibility around these principles? How will you apply the guidelines in your personal life?

What additional guiding principles might you suggest?